Praise for Lead

"I meet many authors and read many books, I love to meet an author who has lived his content before he shares his book. When I learned that Paul was going to write a book on perseverance, I was immediately excited. Effective leadership centers on perseverance. You will know more about perseverance and press on in a more intentional way after reading this book."

— **Mark Cole**, CEO,
John Maxwell Company

"*Leaders Press On* is not written from the perspective of theory but from the perspective of practice… Paul takes you on a journey and equips you with the practical tools so you too can persevere."

— **Daniel Floyd**, Senior Pastor,
Lifepoint Church (a multisite church),
Author of *Living the Dream*

"*Leaders Press On* is a must-read for people who want to bring about a significant transformation within an organization, community, workplace, or personal life… This book is an excellent tool for managers, executives, or anyone looking to make a positive change in their lives. The lessons are well thought out, and easy to read and follow."

— **Paul Martinelli**, President,
John Maxwell Team

LEADERS PRESS ON

"I was thrilled to receive an advance copy of *Leaders Press On* and even more delighted while reading it on a cross country flight... Paul's emphasis on perseverance, a vital leadership characteristic, resonated strongly with me. *Leaders Press On* is well written, and packs a punch on an important subject."

— **Ed DeCosta**, Executive Coach,
Author of *Ascend,* and *Release Your Superhero*

"Leaders are made, not born. *Leaders Press On* provides fabulous concepts, stories and steps to be the leader you wish you had."

— **Stephen Shedletzky**, Founder, InspirAction,
Head Engagement Officer,
Simon Sinek's *Start With Why*

"Paul does a phenomenal job in *Leaders Press On* capturing an authentic journey of a true leader. He unlocks the power of perseverance and brings truth to what a leader must face and overcome in order to make the impact they set out to make. This book is a great resource for all leaders at all levels."

— **Melissa V. West**, Executive Coach, Xtreme Results,
Author of *Your Daily WOW*

Leaders
Press On

Discovering the Power
of Perseverance

To MB
Thanks for believing
in us all, those
years ago!
Keep leading!
Keep inspiring!
Keep press on!

Paul Gustavson

PAUL GUSTAVSON

Phil 3:12-14

Leaders Press On – Discovering the Power of Perseverance
by Paul Gustavson
Published by LEAD EDGE PRESS

LEAD EDGE PRESS
c/o SimVentions
100 Riverside Parkway, Suite 123
Fredericksburg, Virginia 22406

Cover design by Rupa Limbu

ISBN: 978-0-9976872-0-0

First Edition
Version 1.0 - June 2016

Dedication

The greatest legacy one can pass on... is not money or other material things accumulated in one's life, but rather a legacy of character and faith.

Billy Graham

This book is dedicated to my two sons, Ryan and Michael, and is written in memory of my dad, Captain Arthur R. Gustavson, US Navy (Retired). With this book, my hands are held wide connecting past and future.

Contents

Foreword

If I heard him say it once, I heard him say it a thousand times, "greatness is not determined by what you have or achieve, but by what it takes to make you quit." These were the words of my university president, which have been forever etched into my mind and my heart. I didn't know at that time how valuable those words would become, as I set out to pursue dreams of my own. However, I quickly learned the unequaled value in that principle.

Some have said that success is largely influenced by one's pedigree, education, talent, opportunity, or just plain luck. When in reality, if you were to dissect success, under the layers of the obvious lay the most valuable characteristic any leader could possess and that's perseverance. It's the difference maker between good and great. It's the characteristic that allows those with less talent and opportunity to outpace those who seem to have it all. It's the one thing you can't lead without.

That is why you need this book. *Leaders Press On* is not written from the perspective of theory but from the perspective of practice. Paul has helped build a highly successful business in a highly competitive environment. He gives you the pleasure of bringing you behind the curtain to the place every leader really wants to see. The moments when you're scared, the moments when you're unsure, the moments when you doubt you can go on. Paul takes you on a journey and equips you with the practical tools so you too can persevere.

LEADERS PRESS ON

Use this book as your personal mentor. Read it, glean from the experiences of others, allow it to fuel your vision, and above all else, NEVER QUIT!

Daniel Floyd
Senior Pastor, *Lifepoint Church*
Author of *Living the Dream*
@DanielFloyd

Epigraph

But one thing I do: Forgetting what is behind and straining toward what is ahead, I press on toward the goal to win the prize...

The Apostle Paul

Introduction -
The Starting Line

Always run through the line!

Scott Overall

It was the day after the Fourth of July. The headline read, "Runner loses Peachtree 10K after celebrating too early." The story and the picture grabbed my attention. A runner wearing a patriotic American shirt is holding up his left hand as he nears the finish line. His finger is pointing to the sky signifying his triumphant win in Atlanta's Peachtree Road Race. The only problem is that he hasn't crossed the finish line yet. He's still a few steps away.

Unbeknownst to him, a British runner catches him right at the finish and breaks the tape first, winning by 9/100ths of a second.

There are two viewpoints in this story. One is of a man who could have won it all, but hesitated for just a moment. The other is a story of a man who didn't give up—who seemed certain to lose yet persevered to the end and won it all.

You never know how it's going to end.

Hours after the race, the British runner, Scott Overall, took a moment to publicly celebrate his triumphant victory with the following tweet, "Pleased to take the win today at the Peach tree 10km. Always run through the line!" [1] His message is simple, but powerful.

Interestingly enough, there are two lines in every race—the starting line and the finish line. To persevere you need to cross over both, but you can't get to the finish line until you cross the starting line.

The starting line represents where you are right now—it is your present reality. Often, we hesitate to cross the starting line. We are either comfortable with where we are, or we too afraid of the unknown.

Yet, the finish line represents our dreams and aspirations—it is what we long for. The distance measured from before the starting line to after the finish line—between the present and your future—is perseverance.

I believe every person in business and life can learn to persevere and reach the finish line by making simple, but impactful, mindset choices. This book is written for those who want to lead and lead well. It explores the mindset choices we all have available to take action and press on toward a common goal and mission.

Unlocking Perseverance

The pages before you started as journal entries. At the time, I was reflecting on the lives and stories of others, as well as my own experiences. I wanted to capture the essential truths about the power of perseverance; the means and mechanisms that it takes to get through the challenges and struggles that we all face— especially those who lead.

I wondered, "How did the greats do it? How did those before us do it? And how can I do it?" In those lives and stories that I studied, I noticed common patterns of perseverance often against a backdrop of grief and pain. Each story and experience seemed to prove and confirm that these patterns that leaders make are what help them overcome adversity and push through the challenges. They are principles—and they are choices—that any one of us can make to lead ourselves and lead others!

I learned many of these principles from my dad. My father was proud of his service in the United States Navy, and equally proud to serve his church and community. He was a man of faith who always strived to persevere. To him, leadership was about serving, and he believed life as well as leadership requires perseverance.

Shortly after he passed away, I begin to think about the principles he talked about and modeled and how they ought to be shared. I wished he had captured the principles and his lessons learned in written form so that they could have been passed down to others. It didn't occur to me until later that perhaps I should be the one to capture the principles and pass them on. Because of that mind shift, those journal entries evolved into this book. They are principles meant to be shared.

The Proposition

I strongly believe that leadership involves knowing how to persevere from the starting line to the finish line and involves bringing others with you. Each of us should strive to learn and understand the principles to perseverance; they can be a difference maker for those who want to get past the starting line and reach the finish line! These principles are the backbone for effective leadership.

3

It's my hope that the collective thoughts and experiences described in the pages ahead offer you clear and actionable mindset choices to help you persevere.

Perseverance Defined

Perseverance is the continued effort to do something or achieve something despite difficulties, failure, or opposition. Difficulties, failure, and opposition aren't very fun, but perseverance itself is something that attracts us. Often we marvel at it when we see it exhibited, whether in an athlete, activist, adventurer, entrepreneur, or innovator. We're impressed by anyone who learns to overcome the odds in the pursuit of a dream or a significant cause. Those who persevere stand out as leaders.

Perseverance is what gives flight to a dream and what unites a team. It's what helps launch a mission, overcome challenges, and ultimately deliver success. Perseverance is what's needed at the beginning, the middle, and the end of a journey. And it's what can turn life from ordinary to extraordinary despite the challenges.

The "X" Factor

We want to know how those who persevere do it. What is the "X" factor that allows them to face the challenges, fight through the defeats, and yet still achieve great things? What is their secret? How do you seize perseverance? How do you make perseverance not something that you fear, but something you steer? What is the key to mastering perseverance? We want to know because deep down we desire it for ourselves.

In an attempt to answer these questions, I began to look for patterns in those who persevere and reach the finish line. I wanted to know the core set of principles that, when put into play, enable individuals and the teams they lead to *press on*.

The patterns of perseverance discovered help give flight to new ideas and allow us to seize new opportunities. They help overcome resistance and create significant movement toward a goal or a mission.

Who Says You Can't?

In 2000, my business partners, Larry and Steve, and I worked nights and weekends in pursuit of the American dream—to own and run our own business. Our focus was building a startup company called SimVentions. I'll never forget the initial collaboration and excitement.

In those early months, as we shaped our dream, we also shaped a mantra: "*Imagine. Create. Explore. Discover.*" [2] We knew that what we could *Imagine* could be made real; with hard work it could be *Created*. We had faith to believe what we could not see, which propelled us to *Explore*. And because of that exploration we were able to *Discover* the impact of faith, hard work, and perseverance. However, it wasn't easy.

Almost Quitting

After the euphoric start that most entrepreneurs have, a funny thing happened. Doubt started knocking on our door. Much of the work that we had proposed and pursued failed to materialize. Soon months turned to years and, by the middle of 2002, we began to wonder if we had chosen the right path. The battle was more difficult than we expected. We started contemplating some of the common questions of defeat that inevitably circle when doubt comes knocking.

"Maybe we can't?"

"Maybe we shouldn't?"

"Maybe we just don't have what it takes?"

Doubt almost stopped us from moving forward. It would have been easy to settle for the status quo—to give up our dream and go back to our old jobs working for "the man." Doubt was ready to rob us of our future. Any one of us could have declared defeat and headed back into the box titled "status quo," but we didn't.

Instead, we asked a different question that radically changed our perspective.

"Who says we can't?"

The first time I may have pondered that question was twenty-two years earlier. The 1980 Olympic Winter Games were taking place in Lake Placid, New York. The world watched as the US men's national ice hockey team was in pursuit of a medal. Yet, they were amateurs playing against professionals. None of the players had been to the Olympics before, and the other teams were more skilled and more experienced. They were facing giants.

As fans, we were rooting and cheering for them. They were the home team, and we had hope. Nevertheless, the critics said they had no shot. As each game got bigger, fear and doubt crept in. The players begin to wonder, "Maybe we shouldn't be here."

Coach Herb Brooks gathered up his team. He saw the fear and the doubt, and spoke these words, "You were born to be a player. You are meant to be here. This moment is yours!"

Like the spark of a match, those words ignited them. It triggered a change in their perspective. "Who says that we can't?"

In what many say was the greatest game ever played—The Miracle Game—Team USA slayed a giant, the Soviet Union. Team USA then captured the gold, beating Finland, another giant.

For my colleagues and me, the Team USA story served as a great reminder for us. Any worthy dream is going to have some giants. We could have taken off our skates. We could have given up if we wanted. But the bigger the giant, the better the dream. Any worthy dream, whether it's starting a business, or chasing after an Olympic medal, requires more than anything else—perseverance.

Deciding to Stay the Course

Once we realized we just needed to endure and persevere, the next step seemed straightforward—we needed to step out in faith and just do it! However, knowing you need to persevere and knowing how to persevere are two separate things.

After a few Herculean efforts on different projects, we quickly realized we needed something greater than our own strength to make it a go. Each of us, as a person of faith, knew we needed to trust in someone and something bigger than ourselves.

We sought solace through prayer and wisdom from the Bible. What we read gave us hope and encouraged us to find joy despite the trials. We knew the testing of our faith was what was developing perseverance, and that perseverance—if we stuck with it—would build us up. [3]

Despite the trials and the daunting struggle to make it a go, the message was clear! We needed to be patient, to stick it out, stay hopeful, and maintain an image of what could be. This was what we needed to do to persevere.

Finding the Pay Off

In early 2003, the perseverance finally paid off. We landed not one, but two major contracts. One of our mentors, George, who had guided us as an outsider along the way and encouraged us to persevere, became the fourth member of our team. The plan began to become clearer.

Soon we began to add other members to our team; they were people who subscribed to our mission and principles of perseverance. These principles are reflected in the heart and soul of our leadership today. Our mantra— *"Imagine. Create. Explore. Discover."*—is the same philosophy embraced by our full team of employees and is part of our SimVentions culture.

I once heard author and pastor Clayton King share, "It's the culture you create that makes the mission possible." He is right. When we sat down to define our mission for our business, we cast a vision for the type of culture we wanted to have. We wanted an inventive work environment based on tried and true biblical principles where we could develop strong and lasting relationships, be technically excellent, and attract top talent. These components of our mission have become a linchpin for our SimVentions culture.

As a business, we still face various types of resistance and, yes, doubt still comes knocking. But resistance is part of the territory. Resistance is there to remind us we are moving forward. The ability to endure the resistance, stand up against the doubt, and maintain our faith allows us to persevere.

A key part of our mission has been returning to that one question, "Who says we can't?" For me, it is reminding myself that I have what it takes, that I was meant to be here, and that this moment is mine.

Designed to Persevere

Coach Brooks' philosophy for the 1980 Olympic hockey team and my experience with the startup of SimVentions has led me to wonder: *What if perseverance was already part of our DNA? What if, as human beings, we were designed to persevere?*

Consider this: you probably wouldn't be here today if you hadn't persevered to some extent—through something. Your very first breath, some might argue, was a result of perseverance. Your first step—perseverance. The completion of every single day is marked by perseverance. The signs of perseverance are everywhere. We should be encouraged!

However, when we think about things—like getting that degree, starting that company, writing that book, launching that project, paying off that debt, or overcoming those hurdles—the challenges might seem huge and insurmountable. But it's all in how you frame it.

What's needed are ways to unlock that perseverance DNA and bring it back to the surface, where it's meant to be. That has been my intent in writing this book. To help you and me be at our best, despite the challenges that sometimes try to derail us.

How This Book is Organized

Perseverance, while it may be hard, is not as complex as we tend to make it out to be. It can be made simple. And when things are made simple, they are empowering.

Steve Jobs nailed it when he said, "Simple can be harder than complex: You have to work hard to get your thinking clean to make it simple. But it's worth it in the end because once you get there, you can move mountains."

Who wouldn't want to move mountains? Perseverance is hard, but the principles to perseverance, once they are known, make it simple.

For us at SimVentions, our story of perseverance is centered on the simple idea of *"Imagine. Create. Explore. Discover."* It's more than a mantra—it's a model for how we think, act, and do. This same model that assisted us in building a business can apply to others in almost every realm of life. The model helps make perseverance easier to understand. And the underlying choices used for each part of the model reflect the mindset you were designed to have from the starting line and to the finish line. They are mindset choices. The mindset choices focus on establishing the right outlook and approach to your thoughts and actions.

The Phases of Perseverance

To help bring clarity to the mindset choices, this book is divided into four parts centered on the *"Imagine. Create. Explore. Discover."* model. These phases of perseverance are illustrated in Figure 1.

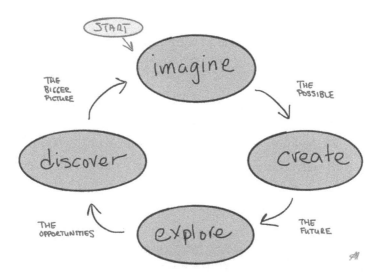

Figure 1 -The Perseverance Model

Each part reflects a different phase of perseverance. Overall, the model provides an essential roadmap to understanding how the mindset choices result in principles that empower us to press on.

- **Phase One** - centers on the choices we have when we take time to *imagine* the possible, and prepare to take action.

- **Phase Two** - centers on the choices we have to *create* the future. The elements of the creation phase include establishing momentum and building a culture of quality and commitment, which are components essential to perseverance.

- **Phase Three** - centers on the choices we have to *explore* with steadfastness. Oftentimes the greatest elements of the journey are when we are in the midst of a struggle.

It's through our mindset choices that we can find our way through and expose new opportunities.

- **Phase Four** - centers on the choices needed to *discover* the bigger picture, which is not just success but significance of the journey. It's because of the choices we make in the pursuit that we discover the significance of our mission, and the difference our perseverance has had in the lives of others. It's at this point we realize the vision we started with was only a small piece of the bigger picture.

Each chapter is filled with stories from my journey and the journeys of others. They illustrate the mindset choices of perseverance, which centers on leading yourself so that you can lead others. They are principles that, if you live them out, can be observed by others and replicated.

Throughout this book we will explore some of the practical methods that a leader can use to help leverage these principles and make these choices. Additionally, we will use a number of mental models as visual tools to help unlock and unleash the mindset needed to press on.

Your Challenge

The premise of this book is that real leadership requires perseverance. It is impossible to lead yourself and others effectively through challenges without persevering. By understanding and applying these simple, yet powerful principles, you can possess the mindset needed to persevere and press on.

I encourage you to apply the mindset choices discussed in this book. Give them a try in your personal life and in your professional pursuits as you lead yourself and lead others. Discover for yourself the impact they can make.

Finally, I encourage you to also be open to sharing your successes with others. The stories you unlock through perseverance can be an encouragement to those who need to be inspired.

Phase One -
Imagine the Possible

The world of reality has its limits; the world
of imagination is boundless.

Jean-Jacques Rousseau

Imagination. It's where it begins. When you think about all the things required to leave the starting line—to get past the place where you might be—the one thing you need is your imagination.

For those that pioneer and persevere, imagination is where belief starts. Before you can create or explore or discover—you need to imagine what can be. Start with an idea, a need, a solution, or a favorable outcome. Now, imagine it possible.

Many of the world's greatest innovations, expeditions, and discoveries were once thought impossible. Consider man-machine flight, electric light, orbiting satellites, man on the moon, penicillin, and a world that is round. It was the few that believed enough in an idea through the power of their imagination to pursue it and prove that it was possible, yet at first they were the crazy ones. Over time, what they imagined that the rest of the world thought was impossible became possible through perseverance. And, by the end, they weren't considered so crazy any more.

Imagination is a key element of leadership. What others cannot see, leaders can. What others do not believe, leaders do. Impossible is a word rarely used in a leader's lexicon. Actress Audrey Hepburn quipped that, "Nothing is impossible, the word itself says 'I'm possible.'" Our imagination is the tool we use to unlock the impossible.

In this section, we examine four mindset choices that every leader can make to imagine the possible.

Chapter 1 -
Start with Hope

Everything that is done in the world is done
by hope.

Martin Luther

It was my final year of college when I hit the wall. My course load was heavy. My grades were slipping. I was behind in my work in two classes. And I was stuck on a project that I needed to finish. It was overwhelming. I wondered if I could make it.

Feeling the pressure, I evaluated my choices. There seemed to be only two: fight or flight. Fight meant for me to just keep going. Stay the course. Push hard through it and knock down the wall.

Flight, on the other hand, would mean for me to just take off. Avoid the wall and flee the scene. The temptation was to get free of the danger—or in this case—get free of the responsibility.

In that moment, I struggled with what to do. The series of events that happened next became a pivot in my life. It is from that experience that three critical actions every person can make were revealed to me. Actions that shift thinking from a stuck mindset to a success mindset. These leadership actions are described in this chapter and are illustrated in Figure 2.

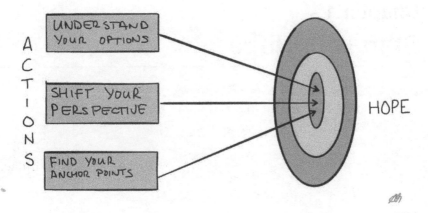

Figure 2 – Leadership Actions Center on Hope

Action 1 - Know Your Options

In that final year of college, I weighed my options. Putting up a fight at first seemed enormous. I wanted to avoid that. I thought, "Why should I subject myself any more to the struggle and the stress? I'm ready to just be finished."

Taking flight was tempting for me. I spent some serious time entertaining it. I was so ready to be done with school. I just wanted to escape from the madness. But, as I contemplated on it further, I didn't like the consequence. Flight also meant I'd be quitting. I didn't want that said of me.

I was just seven weeks away from done. I was so close. "Do I really want to drop my classes and call it quits?" I wondered. "Or should I just fight through it? Should I just stay the course and deal with the stress even though I might fail?"

Those last three words just hung in the air.

The words "I might fail" were causing great fear and stress for me. I had experienced it before, but that last year of college the fear of failure seemed to be crushing me.

I tried to rationalize it by asking a simple question, "What's worse, failing or quitting?" I quickly concluded that if I quit, I'd disappoint myself, and probably never hear the end of it from my family and friends. I didn't want that either.

Fear can be a powerful motivator—especially when it comes to making decisions. In this case, the fear of disappointment was greater than my fear of failure. I didn't want to disappoint the people around me. So I decided to stay in the game and fight!

I took it in thinking, "If I was going to fail, I am going to fail trying!" Making this decision immediately gave me a favorable attitude shift. I felt elated and satisfied—ready. Unfortunately, it didn't last long. There was another fear that I wasn't ready to face.

While I had weighed my options—fight or flight—there was a third option looming in the shadows that I didn't see. I wasn't aware of option three: freeze. Freeze is the default choice if you don't take any action. So, while I chose to avoid taking flight and my intentions were to stay and fight, by sheer inaction I froze. I froze because of another fear—the fear of the process.

When tempted to flee, you have a propensity to freeze and do nothing. When this happens, the fear of the process can grip your mind. The fear of the process is a silent fear that limits millions—including me. To this day, I wince at when it looms in front of me. Process means work, effort, difficulty, challenge, time, and commitment.

19

The fear of the process takes hold when you begin to contemplate the heap of work that has to be done, and the time you feel it might take to tackle it. It can be just overwhelming to think about. The more you think about the heap of work and don't act, the more your mind exaggerates the amount of work that actually needs to be done. When that happens, the fear of the process snowballs—it gets bigger and bigger. This is exactly what happened to me.

I wish I could tell you that after I had decided to fight that I simply struggled with those next step decisions that had to be made. Decisions like, "Which project should I work on? Which class should I focus on?" Yes, I argued those, but truth be told, choosing a project or a class to work first wasn't the issue. All I had to do was flip a coin. Deciding wasn't the dilemma; the dilemma was in the doing. When I begin to consider the work that had to be done, the more I feared and fretted the process.

For me, the gap between doing and done seemed huge! And the longer I delayed, the bigger it grew. Looking back, the realization is that a key factor to perseverance is understanding your fears. Because of my fear, I exaggerated the amount of work that needed to be done. The result became an uncommitted decision.

Action 2 - Shift Your Perspective

Outwardly, I tried to pretend everything was all right but inside I was tearing myself apart. My attitude of unwillingness began to be coupled with an attitude of helplessness. Finally, in a moment of desperation, I did something most hesitate to do. I shared my struggle with someone else. For guys, that's a vulnerable thing to do. Fortunately, sharing my dilemma led to what would be a major breakthrough moment.

The important thing about sharing a struggle is knowing the right person to share it with, and the right time to share it. It requires finding someone who will listen and not judge—who will empathize and encourage.

It was in the middle of the day, and my girlfriend and I had some time to chat for a few minutes between our classes. We had found a quiet spot in the corner of the student union to unleash our backpacks and sip on a Coke. She was relaxed. I was a mess!

She could sense my inner turmoil. "Tell me, what's going on?" she asked gently.

I shook my head. "Nothing," I muttered.

"No, what is it?" she pleaded softly. "You have *not* been yourself the past few weeks."

I took a deep breath and began to let out what had been bottled up. "Alright," I groaned and shook my head in not-so-subtle frustration. "I feel like I am under a rock that I just can't move." I then buried my forehead into my hands and continued, playing it out like a victim.

"I've got something due in every class. Homework! Projects! Reports! Upcoming tests! And the teachers aren't giving me any slack!"

I then added in great frustration as I looked up at her, "You know. It's just so overwhelming. I'll be honest with you; I'm not sure how I am going to make it."

I was a serious mess. Hearing my despair, and seeing that I was stuck, this angel across from me then spoke seven life-changing words.

"But you still have hope, don't you?"

I'll never forget that moment. Sometimes a statement in the form of a question can totally change your thinking. It can transport your state of mind.

Up to that point, I had been a prisoner trapped behind my own bars, but her question blew the jail cell door wide open! It changed my awareness. And somehow I was freed to see a way out. As I pondered that question I knew instinctively what I needed to do. I needed to persevere.

With new awareness, I responded to her question with a nod, "Yeah...Yeah I do. I still have hope!" What that did for me I will never forget. Being reminded of my hope reminded me of my future!

That life-experience all those years ago is still something I think about. It is something that still affects me whenever I feel stuck. Whenever the challenge seems bigger than what I am capable of overcoming, I try to go back and remember that one question. "But you still have hope, don't you?"

The answer to that question every time is, "YES!" Sometimes it's stronger than other times, but a yes is still a yes. Hope can awaken you! It can change your awareness and your outlook. That question, still today, forces me to see something different than the walls of hard work that I might see otherwise.

A key factor to perseverance that I learned from this experience is the importance of shifting your perspective. My pastor and mentor, Daniel Floyd, reminds me that, "It's not what you see. It's how you see it." For me, being reminded of my hope changed how I saw my predicament. It changed my focus from the problem, to the possibility.

By focusing on the possible, our attitude shifts to see the hope, which makes it much easier to take responsibility for what we need to do. For me, being reminded of my hope is what encourages me to persevere!

Action 3 - Find Your Anchor Points

Have you ever considered the alternative if you don't persevere? The outcome wouldn't be good, would it?

A friend of mine once wrote that, "By fleeing our pain we inadvertently also flee our potential."[4] In other words, not persevering keeps us of from being our best—even our partial best. So, why is it that we would flee our potential? Is the fear of pain or the fear of the process that scary? The answer is sadly, *yes*. Fear is what limits us more than anything else.

The remedy, though, is to shift your perspective and persevere with hope. Hope is the spark to get you going. Hope is greater than fear. Both hope and fear park themselves in the same place—your mind. The only difference is that our heart is more involved with hope than it is with fear. When hope is reflected in your heart and mind, you can take on any fear.

For me, this decisive shift that allowed me to see the hope in my heart is an anchor point that I often return to when I'm stuck and I need to persevere. It was a day that I took responsibility for my attitude.

This attitude shift validates the insight I gained from another one of my mentors, John Maxwell. He frequently shares, "The greatest day in your life and mine is when we take total responsibility for our attitudes. That's the day we truly grow up."[5]

It's those decisive moments that can become anchor points to which you can go back to and rev up your engine.

Wrap Up

Hope is a catalyst to living and leading. When you take time to understand your options, shift your perspective, and find a few anchor points, even in the midst of turmoil you can find hope. And when you can find hope, you can identify a plan.

Recognize the anchor points in your life by searching for moments where you made the right decision or perhaps learned from a struggle. What are the moments where hope emerged from the shadow and arose to the surface? Can you find a way to leverage that experience and that wisdom again to make choices that are rooted in hope? Allow them to become anchor points that you can use again to help yourself and others press on!

Chapter 2 -
Cast a Vision

The only thing worse than being blind is
having sight but no vision.

Helen Keller

Imagine the future. Imagine what it can be. Push away any doubt and uncertainty for just a moment and think about the best-case scenario. What is it that you see? What is it that you hope for and want?

According to Albert Einstein your imagination is a "preview of life's coming attractions." It's through your imagination that you cast a vision—a vision that is meant to be shared.

I'll never forget my colleague Bob sharing with the rest of our leadership team the revenue number he envisioned. It was his five-year mark on what he believed we could achieve for our small, yet growing, business. The number looked overwhelming—impossible at first. But as he cast the vision, he showed us the potential growth that could happen for the next five years.

It didn't take long before everyone in the room began to imagine it possible. We carefully explored it from three perspectives: Did the goal fit our overall vision? Did the potential work meet our mission? And would this pursuit fit our purpose? It turned out there was a match! As a result, five years later we hit Bob's mark almost spot on!

Imagining the possible centers on casting a vision. If you are going to spend the rest of your life in the future, why not imagine what you want it to be? Casting a vision can influence the outcome for you and your team. It offers hope. Vision tells you what might be possible. Vision shapes your decisions helping you endure. And vision transforms the present into the future. When there is no vision you risk forfeiting the future. But where you have a vision, there is hope! That's because vision is what gives hope a target!

The question though is *how*. How do you change your focus from your current circumstances to a clear vision of the possible?

The answer to this question centers on recognizing that vision requires clarity. Every leader at home, in business, and in life can learn to cast a vision by attending to three key components. These components are illustrated in Figure 3.

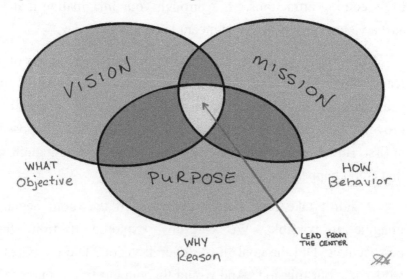

Figure 3 - Finding Vision Clarity

Component 1 – Identify the Vision

The need for a clear objective is the heart of a vision. It gives leaders a target to aim for and can be a source of motivation even in the most desperate of struggles.

One of the best stories I know regarding the importance of casting a vision is the story of Eugene "Red" McDaniel. Red and his family attended the same church my family did when I was growing up in Alexandria, Virginia. Like my dad, he was a captain in the United States Navy. If you've ever met a Navy guy, you probably know they have some incredible stories. Red's story though is beyond incredible—it is inspirational.

Shot Down

During the Vietnam War, Red was a Navy aviator who piloted an A-6 Intruder. In the spring of 1967, he was stationed on the *USS Enterprise* and was just a month from seeing his family back in Virginia Beach, Virginia. However, during a routine mission, a mission he had flown over 80 times successfully before, he was shot down over North Vietnam.

Hours after ejecting from his plane and landing in the jungles of North Vietnam, Red was captured by local farmers and then placed in the hands of the Viet Cong. Shortly after, he was taken to a prison camp affectionately known as the Hanoi Hilton. The conditions were dreadful. Immediately, Red was isolated from other prisoners, interrogated and brutally tortured with the intent of extracting information from him. Red, however, held his resolve. He chose to cast a vision, a vision of seeing his family again.

Prisoner of War

Shortly after his arrival, Red learned of other Prisoners of War (POWs) who were also there with him, but many of them were isolated or in need. Communication was difficult. Red knew they would either live or die, and he knew how important it was for all of them to have a vision of survival. In recounting his story, he shares, "I had to grab onto the possibility that I probably had something I could give to the others that was needed here." [6]

However, communication among fellow POWs was limited. In fact, communication was something that the Viet Cong guards tried to constantly disrupt. If you were caught communicating—or even if suspected of it—you were beaten and tortured. Red, however, would not be dissuaded. Despite the threats and grueling conditions, he maintained his vision and faith and made a conscious effort to find ways to communicate with fellow POWs.

Red McDaniel's story of perseverance as a POW is inspiring to say the least. All told, he moved seventeen times in his six years of imprisonment. Despite the moves and the constant change to routines, he always made it his mission to lift up the spirits of his fellow prisoners. He did this by establishing lines of communication with one another—even though at times he was brutally tortured for his efforts. Red was willing to take the risk because he knew the men needed each other and needed to hold on to hope.

During his six years of captivity, Red maintained his mission by finding creative ways to outwit the enemy. [7] The enemy wasn't just the Viet Cong. It was doubt, despair, discouragement, and dread. And the only way to combat that enemy was having an accountability of perseverance.

Freedom

In early March of 1973, after six years of captivity, he and his fellow POWs were finally released. Many of his fellow POWs, despite being tortured and neglected at the hands of the Viet Cong, walked out of that prison alive because of Red's resolve to help one another persevere. This was a mark of leadership.

Years after his imprisonment and emancipation, I got to know the McDaniel family through the church we both attended. Captain McDaniel, as I called him, was always warm and passionate, caring for others. He is an amazing man still alive as of this writing. I am thankful for men like Red who served our country and protected our freedom.

Lessons Learned

While reflecting on his time as a POW, Red shared the following secret to his perseverance in his memoirs:

"I had to have some belief that I could beat the system each day and that, if I stayed with it long enough, I could live and one day be free. This attitude was to become one of my mainstays in the long months and years ahead." [8]

His vision to "live and one day be free," became his attitude. Knowing that there is a reason for your existence—that you are not where you are at by coincidence—is critical to understanding and finding vision.

The question to ask yourself to uncover your objective—the key element of a vision—is, "What outcome do I want to see?" Take time to work through this question. Explore this in your personal life and as a leader with your team.

It's been said, "The tragedy of life doesn't lie in not reaching your goal. The tragedy lies in not having a goal to reach."[9] A vision in essence is a goal. Work with your team to identify a goal to reach. If you don't cast a vision with your team, you aren't going to get the buy-in that's needed to get everybody on board. Everyone wants to have a voice at the table. So let them share by asking your inner circle two key questions:

- What outcome do we want to see?

- What impact do we want to have?

These questions can help build consensus. And once there is a consensus, you'll have a vision to pursue with the buy-in behind it!

Component 2 – Define the Mission

Don't confuse vision with mission. They are similar but not the same. The objective of a mission is the vision. The mission, on the other hand, clarifies what you need to do to get to where you want to be. It guides you towards meeting your objective. For example, the story of Red McDaniel highlighted more than just his vision, but also his mission.

Unlike a vision, which is time and event limited, a mission can be timeless. A mission can have application for more than one vision. It has reuse value. It's not isolated to just one objective. It can be valuable for supporting other pursuits and endeavors.

Red McDaniel's mission was to lift up the spirits of fellow prisoners by a means of finding ways to effectively communicate and encourage others with his faith. Do you think that mission behavior was displaced after Red and his fellow POW's finally made it out of Vietnam? The answer is no. That mission behavior persisted and became part of his MO. well after his time as a POW. MO, incidentally, is short for modus operandi; it's Latin for method of operation.

Growing up, I saw firsthand how Red sought to lift up the spirits of others at the church I attended and, as I would find out later, for hundreds of families of soldiers who never came home; soldiers that were deemed MIA—missing in action. He has been an advocate for freedom, and his ability to communicate and encourage others is part of his method of operation—it's part of his mission.

Like Red McDaniel, your mission should become part of your method of operation, too. In other words, the behavior you exhibit as part of your mission should become habits for effective living. It should become part of who you are as a leader and how your team simply operates for any vision objective. Companies with a common mission mindset go further, go faster, and go higher than those that do not. That's because mission matters!

What does it take?

Outstanding leaders and businesses, according to Zig Ziglar, "have one thing in common: An absolute sense of mission." A sense of mission helps to answer a commonly asked question for any new pursuit and that question is: "What does it take?" How you answer that question reveals your MO.

"What does it take?" has been a question I have muttered more than once. It is a phrase that often precedes other words that identify a goal or objective. For example, one might ask:

- What does it take to get into shape?
- What does it take get through this work?

31

- What does it take to survive captivity?
- What does it take to launch a business?
- What does it take to be successful?

"What does it take?" is an important question asked by those who want to lead and lead well. Think back to the times when you may have asked it. More importantly think about how you might be asking that question today. If you are not asking that question, maybe you should be. Those that earnestly ask the question "what does it take?"—and pursue an answer—are those who change the world.

The framework for knowing and understanding "what it takes" is embodied by the mission. If a vision identifies a target—an objective—it's the mission that provides a plan to pursue to hit that target.

A mission is what identifies an action plan. It satisfies our desire to know what we should do. We want focus. With a mission, the journey can be clear. And when the journey is clear, it makes it easier to deal with resistance and doubt.

World Changers (Part I)

My list of world changers who asked the question "what does it take?" include Sir Winston Churchill, Ronald Reagan, Mother Teresa, Reverend Billy Graham, Martin Luther King Jr., and Steve Jobs to name a few.

Winston Churchill's vision was imagining a successful conclusion to World War II and the oppression of war being lifted from millions of lives. His mission was "to succeed in doing what is necessary" with "continuous effort."

Ronald Reagan's vision was imagining a strong America focused on freedom, which included the diminishing threat of Communism worldwide and the toppling of the Berlin Wall. His mission, like Churchill's, was "to do what must be done to ensure happiness and liberty for ourselves, our children, and our children's children."[10] Furthermore, he believed in philosophy of hard work to execute the mission and achieve the vision. "If we make up our mind what we are going to make of our lives, then work hard toward that goal, we never lose—somehow we win out."

Mother Teresa's image was to care for the poorest of the poor. That is a vision few would choose. Her supporting mission was to simply show compassion to those in need and share with them genuine hope and love. As a result, she achieved her vision and made her mark in Calcutta, India, one of the poorest regions in the world, supporting the orphans, the poor, and those with medical need.

Billy Graham's vision was imagining the gospel being shared in every country of the world so that its good news could be heard by all people. His mission, as he stated it, was simple. "I want to tell people about the meaning of the cross."

Martin Luther King Jr.'s vision was defined by a dream where one day his children would live in a nation where people of different color and race could commune together, work together, and "not be judged by the color of their skin, but by the content of their character."[11] His life mission, before it was cut short, was to help foster this vision by reaching and sharing to all those who would listen.

Finally, Steve Jobs' vision for Apple was imagining revolutionary, easy-to-use products that offered amazing user experiences. His mission that would support his vision was to be creative by connecting his own experiences to ideas that could influence the future.

Assessment Questions

Here are a few helpful questions to help you, and your team, identify a vision and a mission to pursue.

1) What are you known for doing well? What are your strengths, skills, and talents? How can you use them?

2) What experiences and insights do you have that can help others? How can you use them?

3) What do you (and your team) wish you could spend more time doing? What grabs your attention and interest? What excites you?

4) What new experiences do you want to encounter? How can you achieve them?

5) How do you want to be remembered? What impact do you want to make? How can you make this happen?

Take time to work through these questions and revisit them from time to time. Your answers to these questions can help you find your mission and help you maintain it along the way.

From a leader's standpoint, it's a mission overly communicated and modeled that directs a team towards success. You heard right, you should over communicate the mission. Remember the mission helps answer the question, "what does it take?" If the mission isn't communicated with frequency, then how can it be measured and be expected?

Component 3 – Clarify the Purpose

Let's be honest, a mission statement alone isn't enough. It would be easy to find hundreds, if not thousands of mission statements plastered on the hallways of corporate America, and yet find these businesses not living their mission. Many of these businesses are struggling and dysfunctional. How could this happen? More specifically, why isn't there buy-in on the mission—especially if it's communicated? If people have heard it, how come they don't live it?

While it's true that the mission is what gives vision attainability, the missing piece is understanding the purpose. If there is no clarity on our *why* then the reason to persevere will begin to die.

What you pursue, which is the objective of a vision, and how pursue, which is embodied in the mission, isn't significant unless it fits a purpose. The purpose identifies what you are called to be. Visions will change, but purposes shouldn't. Vision is often time limited. Purpose is timeless. The purpose provides your foundation for each end every vision, and gives value to your mission.

Think of it this way. The vision, which represents a goal or a dream, is what excites you as a leader and the team you may be leading. In business, the intended vision might be a new product or innovation, a new piece of technology, a new service offering, a new set of clients, or a specific revenue number. Vision should be dictated by the ongoing or expecting needs of those who you ultimately want to support. When a vision doesn't allow for change, a business can stumble. Consider Blockbuster, Borders, Circuit City, Kodak, or Radio Shack to name a few. All winning businesses at one time, but the market needs changed. They didn't adjust their vision fast enough. I propose that if their purpose was more up front and center, they would have updated their vision sooner, and they would still be thriving today.

The mission ties the purpose with the vision. It directs you and the team towards a vision. However, it's the purpose that unifies your drive and unites the team that makes all the difference. The purpose gets everyone, including you, on the same page. Without the purpose, it's easy for someone to argue their way out of the objective of a vision and give up on the mission. The key is to know your *why*!

Leadership is the center point of these three areas of clarity. It's the sweet spot of the image reflected in Figure 3. My mentor and friend Scott Fay shares it this way: "Living and working from our Sweet Spot results from intentional design, not accidental disorder."[12]

Lead in the area that overlaps your vision, mission, and purpose. Be sure to communicate these three critical components with your team; allow them to contribute to each part. And always remember leadership is at the center.

Forming a Corporate Vision

I've had the privilege to be part of casting a vision for a company that has been recognized as one of the best places to work in Virginia. That humbles me. And I am honored and grateful to our team for their hard work and dedication. There are many reasons for the success we have had, but the one that sticks out for me centers on our purpose.

Our purpose is "to be a company that honors, pleases, and glorifies God by focusing on relationships and inspiring creative opportunities for employees and customers."[13] This purpose statement reminds us why we do what we do.

Our vision is "to cultivate the most inventive work environment for our employees and be the best provider of engineering services, program management support, and training solutions to our customers." Now, we tried to define a vision statement that had some longevity, but the underlying objectives for this vision statement are evaluated yearly. We call them our yearly strategic initiatives. And we measure our progress by whether or not we have achieved these initiatives.

Notice our vision statement doesn't tell you how we are going to achieve our vision objective. It merely states what we desire; namely an inventive work environment, and to be a best provider of engineering services, program support, and training solutions. Our vision statement simply paints a picture of the future we want to have. This vision statement is inspiring for us, but it's not enough.

The mission statement provides clarity regarding the how. At SimVentions, we put some verbs into our statements to remind us what to do. "The SimVentions mission, which we consider the pillar for achieving our purpose and vision, is best described as follows:

- Seek, and operate upon, biblically based wisdom and principles

- Develop strong and lasting relationships with our employees, our customers, and our communities of interest

- Set the highest standards for customer satisfaction, technical excellence, and employee satisfaction

- Provide our engineering, program management, and training solutions to a diversified set of customers

- Remain a privately held, profitable corporation which attracts and rewards top quality staff

- Support efforts within the local community with priority given to biblically based organizations first, organizations our employees are engaged with second, and general interests third"

Notice there is a reference in SimVentions *mission* statement to the *purpose* as well as the *vision*. That's because mission without a purpose has little meaning. Again, the purpose statement helps clarify the commitment. It explains our why.

Our purpose statement, by the way, took us almost five years to nail down. That's because we wanted to get it right. And now that we have published it hasn't changed—even though we reevaluate it every year. It doesn't need to change because it defines the heart of who we want to be year in and year out. Our objectives though, which are part of our vision, get tweaked every year. They have to change in order for us to be a viable and relevant business. Other businesses can go from good to gone because they fail to reevaluate their vision. But, when you stay focused on the purpose and reevaluate the objectives against the mission that can take your business from good to great.

Forming a Personal Vision

Vision casting for an individual is also effective. After all, you can't lead others unless you learn to lead yourself. The best place to start leading yourself is with casting a vision that clarifies these three components in your life: your vision, your mission, and your purpose.

My personal vision statement—my objective—is simple: "To bring to light actionable ideas, practical insights, and supportive solutions that innovate and create impact." It's a scalable vision statement. This vision statement states *what* I am focused on doing day and day out. The ideas, insights, solutions can be small, or they can be big.

My mission is a bit more prescriptive, yet still simple: "To identify and collaborate on ideas that will add value to others." The mission statement is used to remind me of how I should pursue my vision: "identify and collaborate." The reason why I do it is also mentioned: "add value to others." However, I still need clarity of my purpose.

What is my intent behind my mission and vision? That's where the purpose comes into play. My purpose is similar to SimVentions: "To be a person that honors and glorifies God in all that's been given to me." With the perspective of the purpose, my mission exposes for me how I can pursue fulfilling this purpose and how I can achieve my vision.

The things that I choose to do need to pass through my mission funnel and match with my purpose. Writing this book, for example, has been one of those. Helping launch a business has been another. Connecting and collaborating with leaders who seek to add value to others has been a third. When you focus on your mission and stay mindful of your purpose, you can adjust to new and exciting vision opportunities. I encourage you to give it a try.

- What is your vision?

- What is your mission?

- What is your purpose?

Earnestly work through identifying these three components and, if possible, consider the support from a coach or mentor. Don't neglect any of these components. While purpose may be the most important vision component, start with an objective. That might be the easiest place to start. Ask yourself, what do you want?

Next, work on the mission. What behavior and actions are needed as part of the mission that will help you reach the objective of a vision and satisfy your purpose?

Third, see what falls out regarding a purpose that you can be passionate about that others might want to get behind too. Iterate through all three of these components. Remember that the mission satisfies the purpose and puts you on a path to achieve a vision objective. But the purpose can also stand on its own.

As another example, the vision objective for my wife is "to help lead people towards transformation and be at peace with themselves and their journey." That's her present day goal as a coach, speaker and mom. Her supporting mission statement is "to inspire people to be bold and live life full out." It describes how she pursues the vision, but it could work for other visions too. Third, her purpose is "to be a person that helps others be more fulfilled." Notice that her purpose statement describes what she intends to always be. It's written in a way that stands on its own and can apply to any vision or refinement of a mission.

World Changers (Part II)

If you look back at the list of greats who found success by first casting a vision, you will find they also had a purpose as a foundation.

Winston Churchill's purpose, which he had identified earlier in life, was to "make this muddled world a better place for those who will live in it after we are gone." [14]

Ronald Reagan's purpose, as he defined it, was to "live simply, love generously, care deeply, speak kindly, and leave the rest to God."

Mother Teresa's purpose was stated plainly, "I must be willing to give whatever it takes not to harm other people and, in fact, to do good to them. This requires that I be willing to give until it hurts. Otherwise, there is not true love in me and I bring injustice, not peace, to those around me."[15] By 1996, Mother Teresa and her sisterhood operated 517 missions in over 100 countries.[16]

Billy Graham's purpose has been to live out the great commission. To date, Billy Graham has preached to nearly 215 million people in more than 185 countries. He has reached hundreds of millions more through television, film, and the web.

Martin Luther King Jr. said of his purpose, "I just want to do God's will. And He's allowed me to go up to the mountain. And I've looked over, and I've seen the Promised Land! I may not get there with you, but I want you to know…that we as a people will get to the Promised Land."[17]

Steve Jobs' "think different" mantra reflected just the surface of his purpose. He once said, "Going to bed at night saying we've done something wonderful—that's what matters to me." By the time of his death, Steve Jobs had over 323 design patents. These items included desktop computers, laptops, iPods, phones, tablets, displays, packaging, and even the Apple Store.

In their areas of expertise, each of these passionate leaders was able to persevere through difficult challenges and achieve a great vision. Their success isn't just because they had a core vision in mind and a mission to guide them, but it's because they also understood their purpose.

Wrap Up

If you show me your vision, I will show you your future. That's because a vision paints a picture of the future. It identifies where you can go and what you want to see.

To cast a vision, it's important to have an objective or destination in mind—or else it's not a vision. Second, to cast a vision that's attainable you need to have clarity of the mission. Third, to cast a vision that maps with your values it's important to tie the vision to your purpose. Collectively these three components result in a vision worth persevering. Leadership involves leading from the center, where these components unite.

Every person should cast a vision for no other than these three reasons.

1) To be aware of the *potential*

2) To be aware of the value of the *present*

3) To be aware of the impact of *perseverance*

When it comes to *potential*, who says what you might dream isn't possible? When it comes to the *present*, who says you can't begin right now to influence and change the future? When it comes to *perseverance*, who says your choices won't affect the outcome?

This book is focused on helping you persevere, but if you need help honing in on your purpose there are several great resources I recommend. They include *Start with Why* by Simon Sinek, *Living the Dream* by Daniel Floyd, *Finding Your Sweet Spot* by Scott M. Fay, and *Living Forward* by Michael Hyatt and Daniel Harkavy. All four of these books are excellent resources for helping you cast a vision. Once you have clarity of purpose, always remember the value of vision casting. It's a key mindset choice that helps leaders press on.

Chapter 3 -
Be Bold

Strength doesn't come from doing what you can do. It comes from doing the things you once thought you couldn't.

Rikki Rogers

B e Bold. It's easy to say, but hard to do. The sense of courage that we all want to feel before the journey often isn't experienced until after we get out of our comfort zone. It's in our contemplation at the starting line—in that false place of comfort where we become anxious. We then wonder what it takes to be unafraid.

To be afraid means there is a presence of fear. Logic tells us that to be unafraid would result in an absence of fear. But that logic is false! To be bold means you are willing to move ahead in the face of fear, not in its absence. Boldness can't exist without fear.

To be bold, three factors yield perspective in leading yourself. These factors are illustrated in Figure 4 along with the three entities that are part of everyone's story.

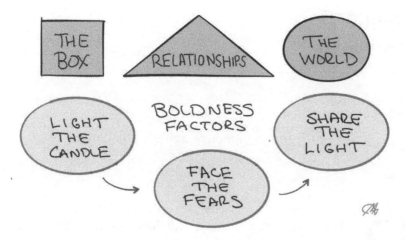

Figure 4 – The Boldness Factors

Factor 1 - Light the Candle

Imagine each life as a candle. A candle that has been created with a purpose. Like a candle, each life is designed to make an impact—to add value to others by providing light.

Imagine though this candle is without a flame. And because of that, it's not fulfilling its purpose.

I don't know about you, but there have been times in my life where I have been the unlit candle, times where I was simply not living out my potential in adding value to others. Instead I found myself trapped in a box—a box often filled with other unlit candles. The only thing is that I didn't know I was trapped at first.

The Box

The box is a place of comfort. It's what you and I would call *the status quo,* or the *mundane life*. For a long time, I was content to live in the box. I was happy with the status quo, and simply followed the script given to me.

But eventually I realized there was much more than what the box offered and I began to get antsy. I wanted to leave.

The pressure from inside the box was to stay put. The sentiment was that the outside is dangerous, too much risk. Like you, I was told that it was better to be safe than to be sorry.

But deep down I knew that my potential would be found outside of the lid of that box. I knew that I was intended for something greater than where I was presently. And I knew my candle needed to be lit. So, I left.

When I got outside of the box, the first thing I tried to do was light my own flame. I thought desire alone would be enough. But a candle can't spontaneously self-ignite! It needs a flame from somewhere else.

Relationships

Eventually, I found others that had escaped the box that lived with purpose and a mission. I was drawn to them. Their flame cast a light, and they seemed to find satisfaction in life. And that intrigued me.

The more I hung around them, the more clarity I began to get and the better my vision became. I began to see things differently. And, because I started trusting them, my candle became lit too! Great connections and relationships can do that. A sense of belonging is a desire we all want to fill. And when you are able to fill it by being in the proximity of others who you know, like and trust, it gives you a new level of energy that you may have not experienced before. It makes you want to venture out—try new things. It is a turning point where you begin to feel alive.

The World

With my candle now lit, and a new passion and energy, I wanted to cast my light. I wanted to go out in the world and make an impact. So, drawing on my own strength, I sprinted down the first path I could find. I wanted to add value.

Then something unexpected happened. In this new world, I met some strong wind in the form of struggle, failure and defeat, and the flame began to flutter. Quickly self-doubt crept in. Eventually I let my light go out!

So, back to the box I went. There I was reminded that I couldn't from the *told-you-sos* that said I shouldn't. And I began to critique myself and question my effectiveness and purpose.

Fortunately, some key people that I had met outside the box stepped in and spoke life into me. You could call it a rescue mission.

They shared that the journey is never easy, but it's worth it. They reminded me the path to success is uphill. That there will be some adversity, but not to lose heart. That there is a plan for me—a hope and a future. [18]

It was from them that I learned that the wind and resistance is something to embrace. They reminded me that, for the sail on a boat, wind brings life. For the eagle that soars high, it's the wind that lifts it up. For the plane that takes off, it is always into the wind. And, as Winston Churchill once shared, "Kites rise highest against the wind—not with it."

I learned from them that the goal is to harness the resistance, not ignore it. Resistance is a sign indicating you are heading in the right direction.

Their words of encouragement raised my awareness and gave me hope and strength. It wasn't long before I was back out of the box and with my candle lit ready to face the world.

Take Action

The flame of a candle is what allows you to penetrate the unknown. The key to getting a candle lit is to get near the flame of another source.

Thomas Jefferson allegedly once said that, *"A candle never loses its flame when it lights another."* This is absolutely true! Those who are candles of compassion listen and encourage. They lean in and they lead. And while it seems they may make themselves a little vulnerable when then get near another candle whose flame is out, the truth is they make an impact. Their flame doesn't go out but instead it often gets brighter.

Candles that have their flame lit, they are bold. They are ready to make a difference and often resistance only makes them stronger.

What I have learned from that lesson is simply this: you can't get strong unless you first be bold. Boldness isn't dependent on a feeling, it's dependent upon action. Don't wait to feel bold, be bold.

1) Be Bold by getting out of the box. Know that you were made to make an impact.

2) Be Bold by getting near the source of another flame. Know where to go to get your candle lit and keep it lit.

49

3) Be Bold by harnessing resistance. Know that success is often disguised in adversity. When you face it, don't give up. You may be closer to your goal than you realize!

The only thing that truly stops boldness is our fear. The next factor is to learn how to face those fears.

Factor 2 - Face the Fears

Head back to the box for a moment. Think about what it is like. There is comfort, but it is false. There is euphoria, but it is a disillusion. There is conversation, but it is stale. Yet just outside the box awaits a menace—or so we are told.

Those in the box sense him lurking; however, he's never truly been seen. Still, we are afraid we might confront him. We believe he's poised and ready to jump on us. Ready to ruin the day!

Despite never being seen (except maybe in an Allstate commercial!) he is not nameless. This menace is known by many names: Trouble, Mayhem and Misfortune to name a few. He is the embodiment of Murphy's Law; there to ensure that if you do get out of the box, "what *can* go wrong *will* go wrong."

It's been said "the best laid plans of mice and men often go awry, and leave us nothing but grief and pain." [19] In the circles we frequent, we might picture the menace with two ugly heads known as "Grief and Pain." Over time, we fall into a trap of believing an often-quoted statement from an old poem as truth, but it's not. It's a lie! The "best laid plans" don't go awry unless they are not acted on.

The grief I'm describing isn't the type of grief experienced with the loss of someone or something in your life. Grief in the context of this discussion refers to trouble, annoyance, irritation, and, certainly, it can evolve into sorrow, misery, and anguish.

Grief and Pain is something we want to avoid—and, because we know it can happen, we fear it! But what if Grief and Pain is more certain for those that don't plan and don't do anything than those who do?

Isn't it true you often get what you expect? If there is a great fear about what you might find outside of the box, then you are more prone to find it. And when you spot it—or at least you think you sense it—it might cause you to stumble and fall. It will likely produce (brace yourself) grief and pain.

What we need instead is a change of perspective. And a good question might be all that's needed to realign your view. My question is this: "Why is it that you settle for what you currently have, rather than what you could have? It's a question I asked of myself, which drove me to get out of the box.

Instinctively we know that if we get out of the box, then there's more to life. But what stops us is the menace, or at least the threat of what he might bring. When you get right down to it, it's the fear that ultimately stops us!

The fear of Grief and Pain is the real menace in our lives. And this fear has us thinking there is safety in the box—in the comfort zone. It's those fears that keep us right where we are at—they keep us at bay. Truth be told, there might be more Grief and Pain inside the box than outside of it. If we could only recognize that the source of the menace is often ourselves.

Consider that often we are the ones that self-sabotage our pursuits. While we might show excitement and enthusiasm at the start, at the first sign of conflict and in the midst of fear we might flinch, think we might not have what it takes, and we might quit.

The real grief and pain results from a vision that goes unfulfilled because we never left the box. A future imagined never pursued will leave you with regret and disappointment. Whereas a future imagined relentlessly pursued results in experience valued and treasured.

The best laid plans don't always need to end in grief and pain. Instead, rewrite the poem. The best laid plans are those that are followed by try and triumph—separated only by a little umph.[20]

Consider ahead of time that any grief and pain you might experience is there to see how much you truly want it. If everything were easy what would be the point? Remember, "strength doesn't come from what you can do. It comes from overcoming the things you once thought you couldn't" [21]

What the Victors Would Say

The great news is there are examples of others who have gotten out of the box—others who have faced their fears and found success. We wonder, how is it that they've found a way past the rhetoric of the menace—of themselves—and achieved their potential? We are drawn to their story because we want to experience the triumph too!

Besides yourself, a source of the menace might also be those in the box with you. If you look around on the inside, you might find that there are those around you who are not victors but victims. They have not yet experienced life to the fullest, yet they are the ones claiming to have "our best interest at heart." They warn us and keep us from leaving the comfort of the box. As a consequence, we forgo the potential victories that can only be discovered on the outside.

However, for those that have left, if they could step out from history and share with you their experience, what do you think they would say?

Robert Frost, an esteemed poet who left the box, would tell you, "Freedom lies in being bold." He would encourage you to leave the box.

George Washington would tell you that leaving the box may make you feel alone, but "'tis better to be alone than in bad company."[22] That's because there's more bad company in the box than outside of it.

Thomas Jefferson would tell you that, "the creator has made the earth for the living, not the dead." [23]And he'd encourage you to get out of the box. He might also add, "I like the dreams of the future better than the history of the past." That's because the box is neither focused on the present nor the future—it finds comfort (and often discomfort) in the history of the past.

Benjamin Franklin would tell you that leaving the box is the only way to write your story, and to "either write something worth reading, or do something worth writing." He's telling you and me to dream and take action.

Fast forward two-hundred and forty years later, Steve Jobs, who also left the box, might tell you that "your time is limited, so don't waste it living someone else's life. Don't be trapped by dogma — which is living with the results of other people's thinking."[24]

Jobs might also tell you, "Don't let the noise of others' opinions drown out your own inner voice. And most important, have the courage to follow your heart and intuition." He is telling you not to worry about the menace—instead, leave the box.

The legendary actor John Wayne would tell you that, "Courage is being scared to death but saddling up anyway."[25] A person of boldness starts by being that person willing to get out of the box and take action despite being scared. The key is to let go of the grip of the menace and take control of the fears and limiting beliefs.

The Twelve Fears

So what are the fears we might encounter that we believe might lead us to Grief and Pain?

All told there are twelve significant types of fears that can dissuade you and me. Twelve fears that might keep us from leaving the familiar, yet false comfort of the box and keep us from persevering.

1) **The Fear of Adversity** – Being afraid of the difficulty, hardship, turmoil, or danger that we might eventually face.

2) **The Fear of Conflict** – Being afraid of the disagreement, battles, or struggles that we might face with others.

3) **The Fear of Change** – Being afraid of the unknown future, facing something new, or leaving the comfort zone.

4) **The Fear of the Process** – Being afraid of the commitment, effort, work, or time required to

complete a job or finish a journey. This is one that has robbed me more times than I can count. This can create that sense of being overwhelmed.

5) **The Fear of Rejection** – Afraid of being put down, judged, criticized, or ridiculed. This is a fear we all have silently faced.

6) **The Fear of Vulnerability** – Afraid of being revealed, being exposed, being found out as somebody who is weak or less than ideal.

7) **The Fear of Being Alone** – Being afraid of loneliness, not belonging.

8) **The Fear of Pain (or Injury)** – Being afraid of getting injured, getting hurt (or getting hurt again if it has happened before), or experiencing agony.

9) **The Fear of Failure** – Being afraid of failing, messing up, not being perfect, not getting it right.

10) **The Fear of Success** – Being afraid of the responsibility, attention, or the change that might happen if we are successful.

11) **The Fear of Disappointment** – Being afraid of not living up to the expectations of ourselves or others.

12) **The Fear of Death** – Being afraid of doing something—making a decision—that proves to be fatal.

Contrary to popular belief, fear in itself is not really bad. It's intended to protect us; make us think before we act. Fear lets us know that there may be some danger if we choose to proceed. What's fatal isn't the fear; it's often our choice in response to the fear. When fear limits our movement forward, then we lack courage. The key thing to remember is courage is a choice not a feeling. And our choices in the midst of fear have more of an impact than our feelings that we might experience. Therefore, choose to be bold right from the start. When you choose to be bold, you will find the strength to overcome the fears you face.

Factor 3 - Share the Light

Once you are outside of the box—out of your comfort zone— fear might still linger and try to grab a hold of you if you aren't careful. But at this point the fears are no longer paralyzing because you are now in motion. The right choices tame our fears, whereas the wrong ones feed our fears. The fears that you might feel are natural conditions experienced for anyone fully engaged in a real world journey. However, in these moments, be aware! The box might seem to be calling you back. The deceptive comfort of the box is tempting, but it's at this point you should seek light. You need a source of energy. Just as a candle needs to have its flame lit to be effective, the same is true for you and me. The only way for this to happen is to get near the source of another flame—get near a mentor or friend who can pour courage into you. Find someone who believes in you and who knows something about fighting through the fears in creating experiences worth remembering.

One of my earliest mentors, who inspired me and poured courage into me, was Bill Kompare. Bill was an area Young Life leader for my local high school, and also the campus leader for Fellowship of Christian Athletes (FCA) in the Alexandria area of Northern Virginia. My family had known Bill for quite some time.

Through his interaction with my brother and sister before me, he became a friend of the family, and was often a regular weekend dinner guest.

When I became a high school student, I plugged into the Young Life clubs that he led weekly and his Wednesday breakfast events called Campaigners. Campaigners was held at different student's homes before school. It was in those Campaigners events and in my one-on-one time that Bill continually challenged and encouraged me to get out of the box and live a life that added value to others. He showed me how I could do this at school, on my sports teams, at home, and when I was in the work place. The greater impact is that he modeled and espoused the words through his character. This could be seen through his empathy, care, and commitment. Bill was the boldest, humblest, and passionate guy I knew. He loved to help people and share the light he had. He made each person he met felt heard and understood. If you asked him for advice, he would give it to you, but not unless you asked.

Wrap Up

Your life is like a candle. It's either lit or it's not. Light the candle. Let it burn. Candles that give light are bold and strong. They live outside of the box—despite the fear.

Remember also that leaders never lead alone. They are part of something bigger. If you need support, look for the encouragement of others. Look for the people in your life like a Bill Kompare. Look for them. They are there. They'll help you persevere. They'll share their light. They understand that one person's life is meant to light the candle of another.

Every business, every organization, every team should look for ways to support one another—to share the light. You are either a source of light or a candle in need of one. Be bold by either sharing your light with another, or by finding the light from someone else who can help you see more clearly. These are the teams and organizations that stand out above the rest. Be bold. Be strong. It's the mindset choice that neutralizes fear, smashes your limited beliefs, and helps you press on.

Chapter 4 -
Believe What You Do Not See

Faith is to believe what you do not see; the reward of this faith is to see what you believe.

Saint Augustine

In the movie *Déjà Vu*, the main character Doug Carlin, played by actor Denzel Washington, poses a question that affects the outcome of the story. "What if you had to tell someone the most important thing in the world, but you knew they'd never believe you? What would you do?"[26]

The person he is asking, Claire, is confused and scared. She has been under extreme duress, and her future is in doubt. However, the question, as great questions do, causes her to pause just long enough to consider life beyond the present. And so she replies, "I'd try! You never know what someone might believe."

Like many of us, Claire is desperate for hope. Great questions unlock awareness. And her response to the question is telling. She wants to find something to believe in —something different that will light her candle. Because of her response, she puts her trust in Carlin allowing her imagination to pivot from doubt to faith.

I find this element of the story fascinating. The change in her demeanor is dramatic. Hope is always worth pursuing. And hope comes to life through perseverance triggered by a shift in the imagination. Imagine the possible; it's what renews belief and produces faith.

Is your story similar to Claire's? I know for me, there have been times I've faced despair, doubt, discouragement, dread, disappointment, disillusion—you name it—but somehow, I'm still here. The fears I've experienced pale in comparison to the hope that I am able to imagine. The key is to imagine, because vision fuels hope!

Every one of us, no matter what state of life we are at, or where we are in the pecking order of leadership, can take five simple faith steps that will transform our faith– and our life. These belief steps are illustrated in Figure 5.

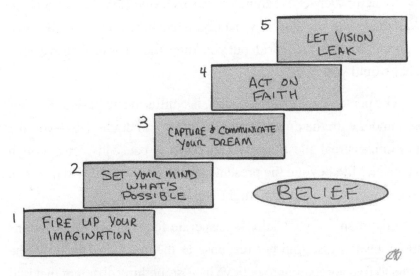

Figure 5 – Belief Steps

Step 1 - Fire Up Your Imagination

Perseverance is a matter of seeing what you believe is possible and going forward through the challenge that you may be in. Perseverance requires your imagination to be fully engaged. It's the essence of faith.

Einstein once shared that "Imagination is more important than knowledge." I'm guessing you have probably heard this before, but what you might not have heard is his reason behind his belief. His rationale is that, "knowledge is limited to all we now know and understand, while imagination embraces the entire world, and all there ever will be to know and understand."

Consider his thought for a moment. Einstein is stating essentially that imagination is one of the most powerful tools in your toolbox—it's greater than knowledge. Knowledge is all that we know in the present. Imagination is what we know is possible in the future. Think of Jules Verne, whose science fiction writings in the nineteenth century were captured in books like *Twenty-Thousand Leagues under the Sea* and *From the Earth to the Moon*, imagined such things as electric-powered submarines, solar-powered spacecraft, Taser guns, video conferencing, newscasts, and skywriting.[27] These verbal images were imagined long before their production and use. Think also of Leonardo da Vinci who imagined the helicopter, the anemometer (an instrument for measuring the speed of wind), and the parachute almost 500 years before their creation.[28]

It's the power of your imagination that invokes your faith – the faith to do something, see something, or be something that doesn't yet exist in the present. The writer of the book of Hebrews shares that, "Faith is being certain of what we hope for and sure of what we cannot see." Without faith, imagination is just a wish. But with faith, your imagination gives hope a chance.

Step 2 - Set Your Mind on What's Possible

Imagination can be fueled either by faith or doubt. But only one of these sources is worth consideration. When our imagination is fueled by faith it yields hope. Otherwise, without faith we live with doubt. Doubt is the menace of faith. Doubt wants to steal and rob, and it will leverage your imagination to pull you down.

The key to this step is to set your mind on what's possible. Success is predefined by what you hope for, therefore let your imagination be fueled by a faith in a successful outcome.

In the scriptures, the writer of the book of James shares that when you imagine, which is reflected by what you ask and pray, "you must believe and not doubt, because the one who doubts is like a wave of the sea, blown and tossed by the wind."[29] In other words, you must set your mind on what's possible. Believe that somehow it will work out in the end. Hope is the prerequisite to success. Conversely, success, real success, is the conclusion to hope.

Pope John XXIII expresses it best, "Consult not your fears but your hopes and your dreams. Think not about your frustrations, but about your unfulfilled potential. Concern yourself not with what you tried and failed in, but with what it is still possible for you to do."

Step 3 - Capture and Convey the Dream

So what is the action needed to leverage our imagination so that we can choose to lead with faith?

For me, I find it's important to take what I have imagined and write it down—capture it somehow! I share some practical methods for capturing a vision later in Chapter 6. But the effect of capturing what you hope for, is that it gives you awareness in identifying the doors and opportunities that might take you towards your vision.

Once desired intentions and hopes have been captured, the next step is to convey what's been imagined to at least one other person. I like to vet it with someone, usually my wife, or a colleague at work, or a coach or mentor. I want to get their perspective, their buy-in, and their support. But more importantly, because I am a person of faith, I need to pray over it. In that contemplation and prayer, I try to ask, "Is this thing that I am beginning to imagine ——that I am hoping for—part of the plan? Is this something I should or shouldn't pursue? How does it fit the purpose and mission for my life?"

If I don't go through this exercise and deposit my dreams through prayer and meditation, then often the dream I've imagined is simply lost and forgotten. Faith expressed through prayer and meditation gives me a place to submit my dream and vision. It's a lot like a writing letter; the letter is only valuable and impactful if it's sent to someone and received. What good is an unsent letter? It has no value to others or yourself. But expressed intent that's received is always more potent than wishful thinking. That's because expressed intent reveals commitment, clarifies focus, and creates accountability. Wishful thinking, on the other hand, is like trying to hold water in the palm of your hands. There's no containment, and soon it slips through your fingers and evaporates.

Step 4 - Act on Faith

Until now, had you given much thought to how your imagination and faith are tied together? Contemplate on this further. Think about the stories in your own life where faith was fueled because of your imagination!

The story of SimVentions is one that started in our imagination—and not just once. It seems each of SimVentions' growth spurts and milestones have been precipitated by us coming together and just taking time to imagine. We try to think of a vision that makes sense with our purpose and our mission. Some of these visions are crazy—at first they seem out there—but we whittle and work on it. Once we can picture it on our mind it becomes something for which we can pray on—and act on.

Remember our mantra: *"Imagine. Create. Explore. Discover."* I can argue that everything that has ever been intentionally created is essentially created twice. Once in the imagination, and then through perseverance, hard work, and faith it is manifested and brought to existence in the physical.

Consider how your achievements and accomplishments have come about because they first start in your imagination. Your intentional actions—and often your subconscious behavior—are an expression of your imagination. All the things that you imagine and desire such as a home, job, business, family, property, car, vacation, boat, event, pet, financial goal, contract, product, innovation, solution, book, movie, championship—they become pursuits in the physical. You imagine then you create. But to create in the physical, it first had to be created in your imagination, or at least somebody's imagination.

The best images I've developed often came through the help of others to see what's not in the present state but a future state. One example was when I learned how to hurdle back in high school, which is a story I will share in more detail later. But on day one, I was awful. Just no good. However, through the help of my teammates and my coach, I was encouraged to create an image of what could be. As a result, I just whittled and worked on that image. My prayer before every race was simply to take what I could imagine—performing well in the race—and transfer it to God's care and feeding. To help me with this, I mentally recited scripture from Philippians 4:13 before every race, "I can do all things through Christ who strengthens me."

Each time I recited that verse in prayer, I was submitting in faith the vision of me being able to accomplish my goal— believing what I could not see. I tried to picture myself not as who I was in the present but who it was that I would be in the future. Thankfully it didn't take long before I began to have some success on the track. What I learned from that experience is that what you imagine is possible if you take action with faith.

Faith, as shared by Martin Luther King Jr., "is taking the first step, even when you don't see the whole staircase." You know the staircase is there, but faith is not about what you can see, it's about being certain of what you can't see. Faith is fueled by your imagination. It is imagination fully activated with the belief that what you see in your mind's eye is possible.

Additionally, for me to fully complete my faith requires the belief that God is able. That there is a plan for me—a hope and a future. When faith is acted on imagination it gives you the fortitude to persevere.

Step 5 - Let Vision Leak

One of the most powerful leadership virtues of all time is written in the book of Proverbs. "Without vision the people perish."[30] In other words, when there is no vision, there is almost a zero percent chance to lead or be lead. Have you ever wondered why that is?

Consider the journey of hope and how it leads to success.

- Hope births Vision

- Vision spurs Imagination

- Imagination activates Faith

- Faith creates Belief

- Belief drives Behavior

- Behavior follows Mission

- Mission spurs Action

- Action produces Change

- Change leads to Results!

Without vision there's no imagination, no faith, no belief, no behavior, no mission, no action, no change, and no results. Vision is critical because it tells you and others what's possible. When you can't see the possible it is very hard to persevere. When there is no vision, it's hard to find belief. And when there's no belief there is little value in our behavior.

Vision gives your mission a target to aim for. Vision must be shared with your team. Leaking vision to those you know, like, and trust is a critical leadership action. Your mission tells you how to share your light, but it's your vision shared that ignites the candle for others. I can't think of a business, team, or organization that's going to have lasting success unless all candles representing the team are either lit, or in the process of lighting others. And that's only going to come by leaking vision.

Remember the words of Saint Augustine, "Faith is to believe what you do not see; the reward of this faith is to see what you believe." Vision is what creates that belief. Letting vision leak is what great leaders do with their team. Share the vision and let them contribute to the vision. Let them own it. Where there is vision there is evidence of hope. Without vision the people perish.

Wrap Up

For my partners and me, the achievements we have had in business have primarily occurred because we have learned to exercise our faith—in the good times and the lean times. Believing by taking a leap of faith results in seeing. I can't tell you how many times we have experienced new sight because of faith. Your faith is empowered by your imagination. And faith is the evidence of hope and trust.

When you put hope and trust in the vision, in your team, and in God, it will change your path and your perspective. Faith simply makes a difference. But recognize that faith needs to be coupled with action! Wait-and-see faith is never the same as imagine-create-explore-discover faith. One is passive, the other is active. True faith needs to be active. Active faith is what leads to achievement. Therefore, start by leveraging your imagination to exercise your faith. Your imagination knows no boundaries. And when there are no boundaries, you are able to think and create outside of the box. It's only outside of the box where leaders press on!

Phase Two -
Create the Future

My interest is in the future because I am
going to spend the rest of my life there.

Charles Kettering

The Future. It's where you are going to spend the rest of your life. Are you ready?

The best way to welcome the future is to step forward into it. As Morpheus shares in the classic cult movie *The Matrix*, "There's a difference between knowing the path and walking the path." Assuming you have been proactive in knowing the path by imagining it, now the next step is to walk the path by creating it. Otherwise if you don't step forward, the future you imagine will pass you by.

Also, creating the future shouldn't be a solo effort. It involves partnering with others who believe in you, who can encourage you, and can help you walk the path as you learn to build momentum.

Like a train that's unstoppable, momentum is the force that lets you plow through the challenges.

Momentum is a leader's best friend. It will take you further and faster than anything else. But you need to have the right mindset for it to take hold. The right mindset will help create lasting momentum.

Author and humorist Bill Bryson shares, "There is something about the momentum of travelling that makes you want to just keep moving, to never stop."[31] He is right. Once you have momentum you want to just keep moving. And creative leaders are always moving.

This section examines four choices that every leader can make to help build momentum and create the future.

Chapter 5 -
Hunger for Growth

Intellectual growth should commence at
birth and cease only at death.

Albert Einstein

To create the future, you need a hunger for growth. If you're not willing to grow, then you're not willing to create. Growth establishes momentum more easily than anything else I know. Growth gives you permission to take risk, and you can't create the future without risk. The risk of growth is always worth the reward.

James Allen, author of the book *As a Man Thinketh,* writes that, "Men are anxious to improve their circumstances, but are unwilling to improve themselves; they therefore remain bound." His comment causes me to wonder. Why is this? Why do we often complain about our circumstances but are unwilling to take the risk to do something about it? Why are we sometimes too stubborn to move?

I believe there are two things that might stop us: 1) our fears, and 2) our beliefs. Our fears can be many: the fear of the process, the fear of change, the fear of failure, the fear of success—I could go on. The other thing that stops us, perhaps more than fear, is our beliefs—especially our limiting beliefs. One common limiting belief is thinking we ought to know how to do something before we try to do it! When people don't know how to do something, they are often unwilling to progress forward—they stay stuck.

A key choice in perseverance that can break us free from the snare of unwillingness is to choose to be growth minded. The desire to grow doesn't require a prerequisite to know the *how*. You'll learn the how as you grow. Being growth minded is what changes your circumstances, it's what improves the culture of a team, and it's what changes the environment on the inside and on the outside.

When we are willing to improve ourselves we are no longer bound to the box. Being growth minded frees us from our current circumstances. It can unleash us from the status quo.

There are five patterns of a growth-minded leader that every person and team can realize for themselves. These growth patterns that can help you persevere are illustrated in Figure 6.

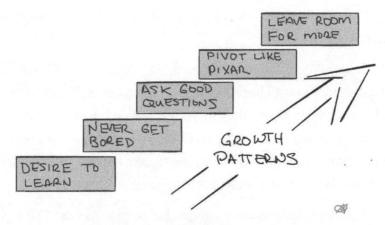

Figure 6 - Growth Patterns

Pattern 1 – Desire to Learn

When I was young, a desire to learn and grow was a big part of who I was. Perhaps this was true for you too. My mind was set on the possibilities of what I could be—limited only by my imagination. While I may have had a dislike for homework, book assignments, and tests, I had a thirst for knowing more and growing more. Experiential learning was the desired choice. I preferred learning by doing and trying rather than reading or sitting in a classroom setting.

If the question was asked of me, "When was the last time you did something new?" Back then I wouldn't have to think too long to find an answer. Today, though, that might be different. I'd have to think a little longer. To emphasize this point, ask yourself the very same question, "When was the last time you did something for the first time?" And what was it? [32]

Is there anything recent that you have tried and done that comes to mind? Or does it take some time to come up with an answer?

For me, my recent list includes the following:

- Using Apple Pay
- Reading a new book on a unique subject
- Trying out a new restaurant in town
- Downloading and using a new app
- Ordering a new and different drink from Starbucks
- Taking a county road that I had never been down before just to see where it went
- Visiting a new country and city
- Taking an Uber ride in London

This question, which leader Seth Godin coined, is one of the most powerful questions I've come across in a long time. It subtly inquires of us if we've grown to be complacent, or if we are still curious and courageous? It's a gentle reminder that a key to growing is to experience and try something new, just like when we were young.

When we were young our intellectual growth matched our physical growth, at least for the most part. Unfortunately, as we get older and our physical growth begins to wane, often our desire to grow intellectually wanes too. When curiosity becomes tempered we choose comfort over courage. When that happens we cease to become who we were meant to be—at least temporarily. Playing it safe keeps us from being our best because playing it safe isn't safe at all.

Philosopher and educator Julia Gulliver admonishes us in this area. "Let us never be betrayed into saying we have finished our education; because that would mean we had stopped growing."

The drive to grow is the fuel that we need to expand our limits and experience our true potential—no matter what our age. For me it's what keeps my candle lit.

Consider that a static mind leads to a static life; whereas a dynamic mind centered on a growth mindset leads to dynamic living. Dynamic living is the ability to process and adapt to an active environment and live in such a way to influence the stimuli of that environment. In other words, dynamic living is about living with a desire to grow.

When you are intentional about growth, you expand your knowledge, awareness, and ability. Knowledge, awareness, and ability are needed to help us persevere and lead. As you persevere, so your team perseveres. As you lead, you instill leadership values in others so they might lead too. It starts with a desire to grow. This desire to grow isn't just an attribute, it's a quality needed for leaders to persevere.

Pattern 2 – Never Getting Bored

Have you ever tried to take on too much—and welcomed it? In the early years of SimVentions, my hands were on everything: developing software, helping create vision, and participating in making every decision. I was helping update websites, running network cables, writing proposals, presenting papers, and publishing standards. It was crazy, but it was exciting. The dream we had to a launch a business was happening. It was real. Our tag line— *"Imagine. Create. Explore. Discover."*—Became more than a mantra. It became a creed I would live by! In those early years, every day that I went to work I was exhilarated. And I thought it would never end!

Unexpected Challenges

In 2007, my father passed away unexpectedly. He had been my mentor, and my go-to guy for advice and encouragement. Now, he was gone. The council that I could quickly get just from a phone call was no longer available.

In 2008, the economy tanked across the United States, but somehow God allowed our little enterprise to take only a small hit compared to other small businesses. My co-founders and I held off taking a salary for only just a short period, and soon the engine of our company started cranking up again. We were able to regain our momentum.

By 2010, we were growing in size, but it started to feel like an unending raft ride to me. The pursuit of a goal had been exhilarating like the peak moment of shooting through the rapids. But now more and more moments seemed like a river ride where the raft kept getting caught on unassuming rocks. It was zapping me of my energy and drive.

For over a year, I wrestled with what was going on. I loved the growth of our company, and I had loved being a contributor in our early growth, but my desire to wear as many hats as I could was burning me out. My effectiveness as a leader began to be in question—at least in my mind.

As I look back, I realize now that I was too fixated on goals and had forgotten the joy of the journey. The first seven years, starting in 2000, while we had goals we pursued, we knew it was going to be a learning experience. Every *try,* whether we succeeded or not, was something to help us ultimately grow and learn. Those early years were all about the journey, about successful failures, so the more rapids and rough waters we experienced, the more the learning. Now, my mindset had changed.

New Year's Resolution

But by the beginning of 2011, I realized I was no longer focused on the journey of building a business with a mission. Instead, I was focused on the management of a business that simply had a cool mantra. I went from vision casting and seeing problems as opportunities, to the routine of producing deliverables, running to and supporting meetings, assisting with proposals, generating processes, interviewing employees, tracking issues, and monitoring profit. I had fallen into the trap of managing a business and wanting to touch everything, and had forgotten the mission of building something that truly added value to others, something that could make an impact.

If you asked me then, I would have told you I cared about growing culture and capability, but I think those things became secondary to me. I wasn't interested in the growth; I was interested in the comfort of where the growth had taken our company. I was, somehow, satisfied with where I was and no longer properly focused on the future.

At the beginning of 2011, I realized that I needed to refocus. I needed to work on my growth as a leader if I was truly going to keep up with the growth of the company. I didn't want to be the one that limited our potential, so I decided to do something about it. Personally and professionally, I knew that I needed a mentor outside of the walls of the company.

When the desire to grow becomes important, doors are opened that help satisfy the want. For me, an opportunity opened up in March to be mentored by legendary author and speaker John C. Maxwell and his team of mentors. It took only a few days to know that I need to step through that door. I wanted to learn, grow, and bring more to the table amongst my peers at work.

Soon after joining his team, I looked for opportunities to connect with him and his staff so that I could learn more of what it takes to be a better leader in business and in life. At one event in Florida, John was teaching about personal growth and how important it had been for him in his journey. That's when he made this profound statement. "When you are growth minded you never get bored." [33]

His statement stopped me dead in my tracks. It was a light bulb moment. Up until that point, I had thought a goal-oriented mindset was the critical key to success in business and life; that we must always have goals, and we must pursue goals. But John challenged my mindset. He shared that hitting goals shouldn't be *the goal*; *growth* should be *the goal*.

According to John, "When we just set goals we might have a propensity to stop after we hit the goals. Then what? What's next? Are you going to rest on your laurels? Or are you going to come up with something else to pursue?"

John paused long enough to let the thought sink in. In that moment, I felt as if what he was sharing was personalized for me. The statement triggered flashbacks of goals I had pursued with passion, but somehow experienced a bit of an emotional letdown in the end. Until then, I always wanted to know why I felt that emptiness after times of accomplishment. Now, the anticlimactic feeling made sense. I knew why. I was goal oriented; not growth oriented. Being goal oriented caused me to focus on the rewards. But the rewards of a goal are fleeting and like the reward points on a Starbucks card, they eventually go away.

I came away from my time with John realizing that when I was growth oriented it had more lasting value. The growth created experiences that would not be easily forgotten. I thought back to when we started the business; there were so many unknowns, but every step toward growth exposed something new. It was in those times where my faith grew and the exhilaration of the journey was in full play simply by being growth oriented. John was right; those where times I was never bored.

The bottom line is that there is more joy in the pursuit of a mission than in the after effect of a win. My advice is this, persevere for the mission and persevere to grow. If you find yourself getting bored, find a growth plan to get you back in the right direction. It will create momentum for you. Remember, when you maintain a hunger for growth you'll never get bored.

Pattern 3 – Ask Good Questions

Today's top leaders, like Elon Musk, Sheryl Sandberg, Jeff Bezos, and Ed Catmull, commonly use goals to measure their growth. It's what allows them to stay successful.

For instance, Elon Musk, founder of Tesla Motors and SpaceX, shares that, "People work better when they know what the goal is and why." Sheryl Sandberg, COO of Facebook, balances the idea off by telling people to, "Look for growth. Look for the teams that are growing…" Jeff Bezos, chairman of Amazon, warns us that, "what's dangerous is not to evolve." But perhaps the most impactful comment to me on using goals to measure growth is a remark from Dr. Ed Catmull, president of Pixar Animation Studios, who discloses his secret to staying sharp as a leader, "I've never stopped questioning." In other words, to set growth goals for you and your team, you need to ask questions.

Questions open up the mind to the possible. Questions are creative in their own right. They introduce and welcome new thought. New thinking yields new opportunities. Furthermore, questions shape how you create the future—and how you grow.

Throughout this book, I have placed questions to be used across the spectrum of perseverance that can help you learn and lead. But the four questions that are perhaps the most important that you should never be afraid to ask, are the following:

- "What if?"

- "Why not?"

- "What's next?"

- "Who's in?"

Those four questions alone will mine more knowledge and awareness than most other questions combined.

Pattern 4 – Pivot like Pixar

Dr. Ed Catmull is behind great digital movies like *Toy Story*, *Finding Nemo*, and *Inside Out*. Catmull is also the president of Disney Animation, producing recent films like *Big Hero 6* and *Frozen*. He has an amazing profile and business resume, and some consider him the father of computer animation. Think of Star Wars, the X-Wing, and amazing digital tools that have led to the special effects of today.

All that knowledge and experience helped birth Pixar. But the Pixar you know today is vastly different than the one that was intended at the start. Their original goal was to create and sell high-end computer workstations for supporting digital animation. Steve Jobs' initial investment in Pixar wasn't necessarily to foster the creation of digital films like *Toy Story* and *A Bugs Life*, but to seed the innovation of high-end workstations that others might buy and use to create digital films of their own.

I am captivated by the story of Pixar for several reasons. While SimVentions is nothing like Pixar in regard to our business focus, there are some similarities. Namely there is a similar desire for a creative culture. Also, there is a comparable path that Pixar and SimVentions experienced that resulted in a change of vision after our respective start.

Early on when we started SimVentions, we had a vision for something quite different than what we ended up being successful at. We had envisioned taking our modeling and simulation (M&S), system engineering, and software development acumen and apply it to create something magical for the first generation Xbox console system. In 2000, we were one of the early companies that participated in what was called the Xbox Incubator program for indie developers, and we begin to get involved as a member of the game developer's community.

Over nights and weekends, we were working on fleshing out a game design and also creating other commercial focused software products and web sites. Our vision was to create a commercially viable game and software for developers and educators that would change the world. The only problem was that we were pursuing markets that we had very little experience or relationships. For us, it was high risk but thrilling. When you have nothing to lose, and you have a novel idea, then it's easier to take that first step in being bold; you just want to see if you can.

For Pixar, when they started they wanted to make computers, and they did! But they had a hard time selling them. In hindsight, they may have been overpriced and underdeveloped. Their attempt at this market, for all intents and purposes, failed, and so they chose to bail.

Likewise, we tried to create a compelling Xbox title but, after getting through several hoops, Microsoft wouldn't buy-in with our concept unless they could physically play a prototype of the game. Because we lacked the resources to create what they wanted, we realized we had to bail. Bailing though should never be considered as failing—not if it helps you move to something better. The key is to learn from it. The experience becomes powerful.

Even though Pixar bailed, they learned to get back up and simply make a pivot. They realized that the software that they developed for their workstations had application for creating digital film, which had already been demonstrated to sell their machines. They realized they had the inside talent and the tools to do what nobody else could do. This realization was the pivot needed to make Pixar, and later Disney Animation, what it is today.

Our failure in producing a compelling game idea also became a trigger for us to pivot and do something different too. After bailing on the game idea, we found some small success with a photography software package supported by Kodak. But we knew that wasn't enough, it was just a stepping-stone. We realized that we had the talent and the tools to support the defense community—a more familiar market where we could interface with our customers face-to-face—so we pivoted one more time. Just like Pixar, those pivots have helped us persevere.

Toy Story Let Down

In his recount of the birth and leadership of Pixar, Catmull shared that the production of the movie *Toy Story* was an act of perseverance. On the verge of bankruptcy, Ed Catmull, John Lasseter and the legendary Steve Jobs brokered a deal with Disney to begin production of *Toy Story* in 1991. The first script for *Toy Story* ended up being far different than the one you and I are familiar with today. After four years of missteps and restarts, they finally finished the movie.

For all those involved, there was a tremendous amount of apprehension once the move was about to hit the theaters. They wondered if it would be a success, or if it would be a flop. *Toy Story*, of course, ended up a huge success earning a whopping $360 million dollars worldwide on its opening weekend. However, shortly after the release, Catmull felt unsettled. The reward of the goal felt fleeting and he began to wonder what he had settled for in life; was it just going to be the grind of making movies, or was there something more? He felt a troubling lack of purpose.

It's easy to become so focused on the finish line and miss the joy of the journey. This happened to Catmull as it would happen to me 15 years later in the growth of SimVentions. Like Catmull, I became finish line focused instead of journey focused.

When I stumbled upon this account of Pixar, as shared in the book, *Creativity, Inc.*, I realized that it described almost exactly what John Maxwell said might happen for a goal-driven person. It certainly mirrored what I had experienced.

Catmull shared that for him the goal had migrated from the dream of creating something special to the act of running a company. Call it subtle goal replacement. This is what happens when you lose sight of being growth oriented and focused on a clear purpose.

I wondered, how many dreams have I started pursuing that slowly and subtly morphed to a mere task for me to manage? But dreams shouldn't be managed; they should be passionately pursued. Management means sustainment; keeping it as is. But that gets old after a while. Soon the dream becomes lost and forgotten and your life's work can become unsatisfying.

Perseverance for the sake of hitting a goal or making a deadline can leave you physically and mentally exhausted. There has to be a greater reason to persevere, something that fuels your tank. There has to be a compelling vision and a mission and purpose.

The idea of merely keeping Pixar running was less than thrilling, so Catmull choose to pivot just as I would years later. For Catmull, he went through a period of retrospection to get at the heart of what really counts. He realized making great movies mattered to him, but there was something bigger at stake that needed to be uncovered to rekindle his purpose and refuel his passion.

He began to look closely at how the company was functioning, and found that the culture of Pixar was out of balance. He realized that they had confused the communication structure with the organizational structure. This created a bit of a disconnect and frustration. The company was off, just as he was off. That's when the pivot happened.

He shared, "We realized that our purpose was not merely to build a studio that made hit films but to foster a creative culture that would continually ask questions."

Once again, when I read this, John Maxwell came to mind. "There it is," I thought. "The key is to be growth minded!" Growth drives culture! When you transition to a growth mindset, your mission is renewed and momentum is created.

Since that strategic shift, Pixar has gone on to create over a dozen blockbuster movies. They have found their niche without losing a step. Consider that if a growth mindset can help a company like Pixar soar, then maybe a growth mindset can help the organization or team you lead as well. It has certainly helped us at SimVentions. And, like Pixar, our culture and commitment to excellence is dependent upon us always asking the right questions.

What Would Pixar's Movie Be About You?

It's interesting that several years after *Toy Story*, Pixar released another great movie, *Cars*. That movie depicts a young car named Lightning McQueen fixated on getting to the finish line and being first. As the movie unfolds, we watch Lightning McQueen realize that the ultimate mission is not about being first on race day. Like Ed Catmull, and myself years later, Lightning McQueen learns through trial and error that it's about the journey and the relationships, connections, and growth that happens along the way. The key is to know that there's always something new to learn—and it's usually with others!

Even more interesting to me is that almost every Pixar movie is built on the common theme of perseverance. It's about Buzz and Woody making it back to be with Andy; Nemo making it out of the fish tank and reuniting with his dad—Marlin; Mr. Incredible making it back safely with his family and learning to embrace their strengths together as a team.

Your turn! Pick a Pixar movie or a recent Disney Animation movie. Can you find the story of perseverance?

Next, what if Pixar was to make a movie about you and your team or business? What stories of perseverance would the world see? What would be the struggles and challenges? What would be the pursuits?

To get you on the right growth path, start by asking the right questions. Here are a few to consider.

1) What direction do you want to go?

   o What are your long-term goals?

   o What's the farthest you can imagine going?

2) What are the struggles you are currently facing?

   o Why do you think you are facing them?

   o Where do you most need to grow?

3) What steps do you need to take to start?

   o Who can help you grow?

   o What price are you willing to pay?

As you look at these questions, it's hard not to ignore that some of them are intended to identify the goals you want to achieve along the way. The goals and steps you identify are important signposts to help measure your growth and your team's growth. These signposts will tell you if you are heading the right direction and how far you've gone.

Asking the right questions is just one simple way to identify how perseverance can unlock the story for you and your team—and pivot like Pixar. That's because asking questions is what helps create the future.

Pattern 5 – Leave Room for More

If you haven't guessed by now, I enjoy studying businesses and reading about leadership. The visionary leaders like Winston Churchill, Nelson Mandela, John Wooden, Steve Jobs, and Ed Catmull—including the nations, teams, and companies that have followed their leads—are able to find a pattern of success by ultimately focusing on a culture of being growth minded. Growth mindedness allows teams to persevere. It allows individuals to look at challenges and failures as opportunities for growth and improvement. Plus, growth mindedness keeps leaders from being too disappointed and becoming too burned out.

That's not to say goals are bad. On the contrary, having goals is important, but a goal-centered mindset can leave you feeling a bit empty and dry. A common example is often what happens year in and year out in the world of sports.

If you are a fan of the National Football League, consider a team like the Washington Redskins as an example. For this team, a growth mindset is often trumped by a goal mindset. As a result, every few years a new coach or a new quarterback is put in place because the last one didn't meet the goal. What if teams and organizations measured themselves not by the goals they set, but by the growth they met? I would argue the reason why the New England Patriots always seem to be contending for a division championship is because there is continual growth within the structure of the team.

Goals matter best in the context of the growth you are pursuing. Instead of focusing on the destination, focus instead on the journey and those who are along with you. Ride it out together, grow together. Always leave room for more. This allows you to work together and win together!

Consider goals as the mile markers along the way of your journey. They are used to identify if you are heading in the right direction and at the right speed, or if you need to straighten the wheel a bit or readjust your rate of speed. The key is to keep moving. Don't stop at each rest stop thinking you are there only to realize later, "Oh, we're not there." Goals can make you stop. Growth keeps you moving. Growth breeds momentum. Growth always leaves room for more.

Wrap Up

In this chapter, we examined five elements to being growth minded: 1) It starts with desire—a desire for growth. 2) A growth mindset will keep you from getting bored. 3) One way to learn and create the future is to ask good questions. Questions are what help you pivot. 4) Life is going to be filled with lots of pivot moments, don't be afraid of them. Consider how you can "Pivot like Pixar", and 5) always leave room for more. As a leader, you can never grow too much. Keep the hunger for growth.

Maxwell shares that, "Growth is the great separator between those who succeed and those who do not."[34] He adds, "When I see a person beginning to separate themselves from the pack, it's almost always due to personal growth." That's because leaders like Ed Catmull get it. They understand the importance of growth. Catmull says it simply this way, "I believe the best managers make room for what they do not know."[35] His comment is the essence of a growth mindset. It establishes an attitude that helps you and others press on.

Chapter 6 -
Activate Systems and Tricks

We become what we behold. We shape our
tools and then our tools shape us.

Marshall McLuhan

I t's hard to create the future without the use of good tools. One of the greatest discoveries for me has been identifying the useful systems and tricks to help me persevere. And I'm constantly looking out for ways to make them better.

In my office, I have a card on my desk that serves as a touch point accredited to author David Allen's work on time management. It's from his best-selling book *Get Things Done*. The title of the card simply says, "Systems and Tricks."[36]

The back of this card reminds me that I need effective systems and tricks to maintain my task list and work to achieve my goals and objectives. It challenges me by asking a simple question. "Do I have systems and tricks in play to help maintain clarity and stay disciplined?"

This touch point is an effective tool in its own right; it forces me to think about my projects and efforts more frequently, more easily, and more in depth. It helps me to imagine, create, explore and discover.

There are three essential systems that can help a leader lead themselves and lead others, as illustrated in Figure 7. I'll explore each of these systems and recommend a tool or trick that I use to help put these systems in place so that I can more easily persevere.

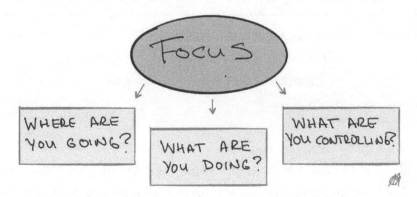

Figure 7 – The Essential Areas of Focus

System 1 - Focus on Where You Are Going

Clarity is essential to perseverance. Chapter 2 emphasized the importance of casting a vision. Clarity gives you context to frame the path forward and the content to paint a picture of the potential scenario and results that you have in mind. If you work to identify personal goals, team objectives, or the business products and services that you and your team want to offer, then you'll gain clarity.

Ideation

A system and trick to *knowing where you are going*—or "remembering your future" as my friend and mentor Paul Martinelli likes to put it—is to ask yourself the right questions. Here are three simple ones that we use at SimVentions to capture our vision, convey the needs of our customers, and to collaborate on our internal needs.

- What are the *outcomes* in mind?

  As Steven Covey says, "begin with the end in mind." This means to have a clear vision of a desired direction and destination. This is about the vision that you have. What are the needs? Where do you want to go? What do you want to create? What's the story you have in mind? What's important to you, and why?

- How does the story play out through *actions*?

  What are the actions that need to be made? The outcome can't be reached and the story can't be lived out without actions. Every action results in an accomplishment. What are those small steps? Consider them as mini-goals. Mini-goals are vital to measuring progress. They help identify the process and activities needed to carry out the story. What are those actions that are important, and why are they important?

- Who are the *actors* that are part of the story?

  An actor specifies a role played by a person or a system that interacts with the story. Actors are agents of influence. Every story has actors. What type of actors are needed to help you and your team achieve your mini-goals and reach your vision? Who or what can help you persevere, and why might they be important? Also, an actor also includes you. How do you see yourself? What's your role?

These three basic questions—What? How? and Who? — often go through a few rounds of exploration. Identifying the desire *outcomes*, *actions* and *actors* provides a simple framework that supports a wide range of visioneering and ideation scalable at almost any level. Think of ideation as a creative means to generate, develop, and collaborate on a vision, project or dream.

I encourage you to ideate and visualize your thoughts by sketching them out them on a white board, a sheet of paper, or on your iPad. Or you might want to use a graphing or mindmap tool on your computer. My friend Nathan calls this activity a brain scan. When you visually see the goals and objectives that you ideate and want to accomplish—specifically the desired outcomes, actions and actors—and it creates clarity and connection with yourself, your team and, if it's a business exploration, your clients. Ideation that comprises using this type of technique spans across multiple stages of a thought cycle, "from innovation, to development, to actualization."[37] There a lot of complicated tools out there that you can use. But most of the time you just need to keep it simple. Keeping it simple removes the barrier from getting started.

Early SimVentions Visioneering

The early days of SimVentions (and still today) our best visioneering sessions for creating the future occurred when we took turns ideating by drawing boxes, blocks and various other shapes filled with words and thoughts on a simple white board answering:

- What could we offer? (What if?) <- *Outcomes*
- Who would benefit from it? (Who's in?) <- *Actors*
- How could we provide it? (What's next?) <- *Actions*

I still have an archive of several of those white board moments from the early days. They literally painted a picture of what we wanted to create. And many of those ideas later came to fruition.

My first experience with this visualization exercise was when my partner, Steve, and I were kicking around an idea at a restaurant in Orlando. We had been inspired by some of the needs shared at a conference we were attending. In the spark of the moment, we conceptualized our idea with the pen and ink on the back of a napkin. Capturing the idea on paper gave us clarity. A few months later, that napkin drawing ended up turning into a full-fledged research and technology project. The napkin captured all three elements: the *outcome* or product desired, the *actions* of how the product would be used, and the *actors* who would benefit from the product.

Today, one of my favorite tools for back-of-the-napkin visioneering is my iPad and app called *Paper* by a company called FiftyThree. With this app, I have a simple tool to conceptualize visually and share with others. I few of the sketches and drawings in this book were created using that app. They are not perfect—they certainly won't win any drawing awards—but they are effective in helping communicate concepts. It's a great tool for ideating a thought or concept.

Taking It Further

Literally painting a picture can be a difference maker. The key isn't your skill as an artist; it's knowing what questions to consider. To help you further, here are some core questions that you and your team can use to visually explore with clarity. Use these questions with your team, and use a white board, a tablet, or similar display technology to visually capture what ideas are generated.

- What *problem/challenge* needs to be solved?

- What *opportunity* exists?

- What *ideas/solutions/resources* come to mind?

These three questions help you identify an outcome. They also help you identify potential actions (or activities) to help you move forward. The first question alone creates the greatest value. My friend and colleague Joe, who is on our leadership team, often reminds us that "the most important thing isn't our need to sell, but our customers need to buy." When you ask the question, "What problem/challenge needs to be solved?" you are intentionally looking to provide a solution to an existing problem that someone has. You are trying to get clarity on the *outcome*. There is a real need and you have to identify it. Whatever product or service you conceptualize and propose as a solution to a customer has to support the customer need—even if it's a latent need—first and foremost.

I encourage you to consider that thought as you ideate. Make sure it's meaningful. This will give you permission to explore. Capture each of these elements (outcomes, actions, actors) as various boxes and circles on a white board, drawing app, or paper. Use different colored markers or different colored sticky notes if you like. As you contemplate on the boxes, circles, and shapes that you use, feel free to reposition them—move them around to gain a perspective on the problem that needs to be solved, your supporting ideas, and the values that need to be exhibited to take on the challenge or problem.

As you next look upon the visual information, ask yourself and your team the next set of questions.

- What *hurdles* and *barriers* stand in the way that might require additional action?

- What are the *distractions* that could keep you from reaching the goal?

Answering these two additional questions will help you to form a clearer picture. All the world isn't blue sky. Know what problems that might exist. You'll find exploring the impediments creates a powerful system and trick for creating connection with yourself and your team, and even your clients. It turns problems into opportunities.

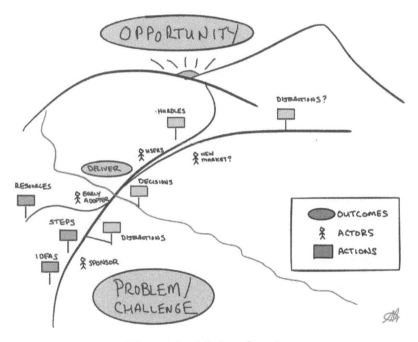

Figure 8 – Vision Casting

To help with the visual picture, one idea that you may want to consider is the metaphor of an open highway with a target destination identified at the end of the road—this outcome is your grand vision. Along the road, place sign posts to mark the journey, which are smaller *outcomes* or *actions*. You may even add forks and turns in the road to show decision points and distractions (as ramps and off ramps), and barriers (as rivers and railroads). An example is provided in Figure 8.

As you begin to explore the environment that you have to work with, compare what's in front of you in the present (today) against the picture you have visualized for the future (tomorrow). The final set of questions you might want to ask are the following:

- What additional *steps* and *decisions* we need to make?

- What *direction* should we take?

- What's *stopping* us from moving forward?

If you don't consider those final three thoughts, then the temptation may be to stay where you are—in the present—and not move toward the opportunity, which, again, is your vision. Having a clear vision drawn out for you can compel you and your team to create with perseverance!

System 2 - Focus on What You Are Doing

Discipline is all about execution. The key to execution is to focus on what you are doing.

Another tool that I want to share is borrowed from the software development world. It is the concept of Agile Scrum. Agile Scrum is a framework for groups and teams to work on key projects in a series of sprints. These sprints are short iterations, usually 2 to 4 weeks, which result in the creation of working software.

Agile Scrum has helped change the game in getting things done for software developers—and getting a team on the same page. I have found Agile Scrum can also be used at a practical level for almost any project. It's not just for teams but for individuals too!

I have what I call a scrum board on my wall both at work and at home. Each day when I come in to the office, I walk over to my scrum board, which is just simply a white board with four columns.

To Do	Doing	Done	MEETINGS

Figure 9 - Leadership Scrum Board

The first column identifies my "To Do" list, also known as a backlog. It captures anything and everything that I can think of that, at some point, needs to be done. If there's something new I need to add, I add it to that list.

The second column identifies my "Doing" list. This list is shorter. I only place a maximum of three things at one time from the "To Do" list on to my "Doing" list. I first try to pick from the list those things that are important and urgent and then knock those out for the day. Daniel Pink calls the first item your MIT— or Most Import Thing. Keeping only three items max at any one time in the "Doing" column helps reduce the amount of context switching—or task switching. The more you switch tasks the longer it takes to get things done. Table 1 illustrates the productivity drop that happens on average when you try to multitask.

Table 1 – The Effects of Multitasking [38]

Number of Tasks	Focus Time per Project (%)	Waste (%)	Total Time on Tasks in a 30 minute period (cumulative)	Amount of time lost in a 30 minute period
1	100%	0%	30 minutes	0 minutes
2	40%	20%	24 minutes	6 minutes
3	20%	40%	18 minutes	12 minutes
4	10%	60%	12 minutes	18 minutes
5	5%	75%	7.5 minutes	22.5 minutes

The table only shows a maximum of 5 items. Honestly, some people try to do even more than 5— they believe they are equipped as *multitaskers*. But look how much time can be wasted multitasking; even if someone is twice as efficient as the average person there is still waste that results.

Context switching takes effort and results in lost time for anyone– no one is exempt. Consider that the more things that you try get done at once, the more the things tend to get only half done. Starting a project isn't the same as finishing a project. And that feeling of overwhelmed can often occur when you have too many things in your "Doing" column. Again, keep the number of items down to a manageable size. The fewer, the better. As long as it's at least one. When you are done, add the next one.

I would suggest also limiting the time you are going to spend on each task. Can you do it in 10 minutes, 30 minutes, or 90 minutes max? Don't give yourself all day. Consider putting a time clock on what you are *doing*. That way you'll get more done, and find more spare time to enjoy other things. Also, consider turning off the phone, the TV, the computer, Facebook, or closing the door. Find ways to focus on that one item in your "Doing" column. Finally, banish perfection– it's the ultimate form of procrastination, and procrastination keeps people like me from getting things done.

The third column identifies the "Done" list. This list is an amazing list, because it shows me what I've accomplished in a short period of time. When I'm able to put things in my "Done" column list, there is a terrific sense of satisfaction, a dopamine hit, which is one of the powerful neurotransmitters that fuels us in what we do. I can then move an item from my "To do" column to my "Doing" column, and began whittling on that.

The fourth column identifies my schedule for the day. This is not normally part of a traditional scrum board, but it's on mine, and I recommend it for you too. I like to visually see my day calendar, and others see it too. This helps me focus on meetings and appointments, as well as dedicated time I have carved out to get something done. Having the visibility of my schedule outside of the frame of my laptop and mobile device has been a powerful way to maintain clarity and stay disciplined as I explore opportunities.

My scrum board is a simple and effective tool that I can use to keep me persevering throughout the day. It is also a tool that I can draw others people attention to as well—to let them know what I'm presently working on and to capture their needs in my backlog that I also might need to support. This is a tool I highly recommend for anyone who needs help in pressing on. The key is understanding how to work each column.

Capturing Your "To Do" List

The questions a leader asks reveals their character and that of their business. And the one question that every leader should ask is, "What can I do to make a difference?"

Take time to think through this question. This exercise might challenge you a bit regarding whether or not you have the right mission and the right vision, but that's okay! If necessary, extend the question a bit if it helps.

- "What can I do to make a difference to fulfill my mission?"

- "What can we do to make a difference to reach our vision?"

What this exercise will do is help identify the pursuits and opportunities that are before you. It helps give direction. You might be surprised by how many items you identify, and how many you thought were important beforehand, but you realize aren't difference makers.

What you identify in the exercise above should go on your "To do" list. This list should contain your wildly important goals that you intend to accomplish, which are focused on a mission. But having a list that identifies the goals to achieve that support your mission is simply not enough.

Next, you need to move what is most important and urgent from your "To do" list to your "Doing" list so that you can begin to take action.

Working Your "Doing" List

A "To Do" list by itself is simply a list of good intentions. However, a "Doing" list is a list of actions that you are presently taking. The point of intentionality happens only once you take that first step on the path. You can't persevere without crossing over the starting line, that's why taking the right action at the right time matters.

For me, the hardest step is going from knowing what I need to do to doing what I need to do. Of all the scrum board columns we've mentioned, perhaps the most important is the "Doing" column. It identifies the current activity you are engaged in the present. When it comes to what you doing, the real question to ask from a leader's standpoint is what are you doing for others?

Martin Luther King Jr. once stated that, "Life's most persistent and urgent question is, 'What are you doing for others?'" This is the question that innovators, pioneers, and leaders should be asking if they want to change the status quo.

"What are we doing for others?" might have been what Rockefeller, Carnegie, Edison, and Ford considered after the Civil War and at the turn of the twentieth century. In response to that question, they forged new industries—oil, steel, electricity, and automobiles—and changed the way we work and live. It may be a similar question that Steve Jobs asked in his leadership of Apple, or support for Pixar. Think of the computer like the Mac, digital animation like *Toy Story*, and mobile devices like the iPhone.

Whether it was Edison, Ford, or Jobs, each of these individuals—
and the organizations that they led—revolutionized industry. They
changed the status quo.

From an organization's viewpoint, King's question can vary
slightly.

- What are we doing for others?

- What are we doing for our customers?

- What are we doing for our employees?

- What are we doing for our community?

- What are we doing to make a difference?

The last question of this list is a variant of the lead off question
asked earlier, "What do we need to do to make a difference?" Look
at your scrum board if you have one. Are there things in any of
columns that are making a difference? There should be.

Name an industry, a profession, a calling, and you might hear
one of this question diligently pursued by those who are ultimately
making a difference. A partial list of some of the most inspiring
companies in America are identified in Table 2.

Table 2 - America's Most Inspiring Companies

• Amazon	• Costco	• Starbucks
• Apple	• Disney	• Target
• Chick-fil-A	• Google	• Toms Shoes
• Coca-Cola	• Microsoft	• Walmart

Each of the 12 companies in Table 2 was identified by Forbes in 2015 as one of America's 25 Most Inspiring Companies. These are recognizable businesses that not only know their path, but they are walking the path. They know what action to take and when. They have a clear vision and are executing their mission.

Even on a personal level this question, "what are we doing to make a difference?" echoes the sentiment that baseball player Jackie Robinson shared almost seven decades ago. "A life is not important except in the impact it has on other lives."

Robinson, through his perseverance, ended up changing the entire culture of America. He was the first pro black baseball player to play in the big leagues. It wasn't easy. But he wanted to make a difference, and that required perseverance by choosing everyday what action to take. Because of that, he left a path for others to follow. He changed the status quo.

This question of pursuit is a question all leaders should ask. Great leaders don't settle for the status quo. They choose a new path. And to lead means you are out in front, and bringing people with you.

If you go back to Robinson's comment earlier and apply it to a business or an organization, it sheds a whole new light. "A business is not important except in the impact it has on other lives."

This perspective should cause all leaders to pause. I know it does for me. Go back and look at the list of the twelve most inspiring companies mentioned previously in Table 2. Why are they inspiring?

I think there are two answers: 1) they inspire because they have a mission that they follow, and 2) they realize their business is not important except in the impact they have on other lives.

If your business, organization, church, team, or school is not making an impact on the lives of others, then quite possibly you might be missing a great opportunity! All of us should ask ourselves, "Am I walking the path?"

To walk the path, you and I need to move things from our "To do" list to our "Doing" list that make an impact. Identify what action to take and then take it. Start by simply asking, "What are the one or two things that I can take action today to fulfill my mission and impact other lives?"

The items in your "Doing" list don't need be long. Just a few of the most viably important ones are all that matter. Remember the mission isn't truly a mission unless there's action, and the finish line only comes for those who persevere.

Celebrating Your "Done" List

The third column is there for a reason. You and your team need to be aware of what has been accomplished. Accomplishments, even the smallest ones, build momentum. Knowing your success motivates you to continue to be successful. But getting something done doesn't mean you are done. Continue to work the "Doing" list. In your "Doing" column, add the next most important thing on the list. Then go work it. Get that also into the "Done" column. If you keep it going, you'll find you can get a vast amount of work done—tasks that aren't just busy work but real value work. When you move from "Doing" to "Done" you are showing yourself and others that you are persevering!

System 3 - Focus on What You Control

At any point of the journey, panic can strike. It's easy to feel overwhelmed. A great trick to regain control and help you create with focus is to practice The Control Divide.

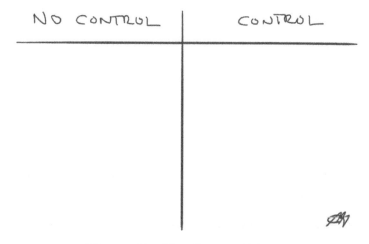

Figure 10 - The Control Divide

The Control Divide was something that I learned from psychologist and leadership author Dr. Henry Cloud in his groundbreaking book *Boundaries for Leaders*. It's a tool to help you attend to what matters really matters, and help you maintain control.

This tool is easy to use. Go to a white board or take a piece of paper, and draw a line down the center of it from top to bottom. You should have two columns. Label the first column "No Control." Label the second column "Control."

Now think of the concerns that you have some significant worry or anxiety about. Perhaps it is something that is plaguing you at work or at home, or in the world news. Write each of them down. You might begin by asking, "What part of my life is simply not in my control, but I worry about?" Take a few minutes to fill the left column with as many things that come to mind that are making life or business difficult. Again, these are the things that you worry about and fret over, but look for the elements of a worry that ultimately you have no direct control.

Before you go to the right column, spend a few minutes thinking over those concerns which you have no control. Are these things that might be wearing you down? Cloud recommends five to ten minutes of really worry time. He says, "Obsess over them. Ruminate. Dwell. Think it through over and over."[39] If there's something you need to add to the column—add it.

At some point in the process ask yourself, *"Why I am letting these things bother me?"*

Next, move to the second column on your sheet. In this column, identify all the things you do have control over, which you should own; those things you are responsible for and you can influence. Cloud calls these items "the things you can control that can drive results."

Again, take five to ten minutes to dwell on them. If there's something else that you can add to the column that you can control, then again, add it. As you look through each of these items, recognize the power you have in controlling each item. Consider how each item affects your attitude. Consider how you can be disciplined to manage only those things that matter. What are you putting off?

After you are done, put the full list away for a day and then do it again. In your mind, identify the concerns that you have no control over. Make it clear to yourself that these are things you have been obsessing over. Admit it to yourself freely.

Cloud calls this *worry time*. Once this exercise is completed after day two, then put a big slash mark down that column to quarantine the items and stop thinking about the items in that column.

Tell yourself this, "I will not worry about what I can do nothing about!"

If one of those items in column one comes back up in your mind, remember that thought: "I will not worry about what I can't do anything about!"

Then focus on the right hand column—the things you do have control.

Start focusing every day on that column. Every day! Make them the priority. If you need to add another activity that will drive results that you control, then add it. But keep the list simply to those things for which you do have control!

My pastor, Daniel Floyd, who I also consider a mentor, shares it this way, "You've got to remind yourself to not worry about what you can do nothing about. Instead influence what you can influence!" If you are finding yourself stressing over circumstances that you can't control, then remind yourself "that's nothing I have control over." However, if you are finding yourself worried about something you can influence, then ask yourself what you can do to manage that area. You'll find that taking this assessment combined with the application of other practical systems and tricks can be a powerful choice that will help you persevere.

Wrap Up

Tools are intended to help you create and keep focus. At SimVentions, we make it our business to design, make, and use tools that can help our customers and warfighters focus. We know that tools—the right tools—can be powerful. But there are lots of other well-meaning tools out there that could get people side tracked—occasionally even our own. The key is to choose carefully the system and tricks you need that will help you persevere. Find others who can help you fine tune and shape your tools. The tools you need should be centered on helping you focus on one of three areas: 1) where you are going, 2) what you should be doing, and 3) what you can control. When you have the right systems and tools combined with the right focus, you and your team will have the capacity to create and press on.

Chapter 7 -
Lead with The Right Attitude

Nothing can stop the man with the right
mental attitude from achieving his goal.

Thomas Jefferson

One of the critical mindset choices to perseverance is your choice of attitude. It's almost impossible to create something good without the right attitude. Attitude, according to Winston Churchill, "is a little thing that makes a big difference." Often it's the difference between success and defeat.

Attitude reflects your integrity. Attitude is an inside out principle. It starts on the inside, but always shows up on the outside. The great thing about attitude is that we can learn to control it. We choose the attitude we want to have, even if our own feelings might push against us. Even when the pressure is on, your attitude is ultimately still your choice.

There are two common habits related to attitude that a great leader that perseveres exhibits day in and day out; habits that you and your team can learn to harness. This chapter expands on both habits, and the representative leadership values we should attend. These habits and values are depicted in Figure 11.

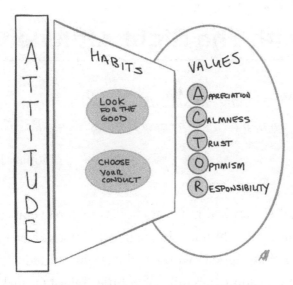

Figure 11 - Leadership Attitude

Habit 1 - Look for the Good

One of my mentors, Roddy Galbraith, once said, "Hope, love, and determination make for great emotions." I have found this to be true!

A few years back I took my family to Disney World. The kids, my wife, and I were excited and couldn't wait for the day. After parking at the Disney lot, we went to the sales counter and stood in line to buy our tickets. Once we finally had our tickets we boarded the monorail to our destination—the Magic Kingdom!

No Admittance

While it was early in the day, the crowd was already in full force, pushing to get through the gate. I approached the turnstiles with a grip on the tickets as if they were the golden tickets for Willy Wonka's Chocolate Factory. Once I got to the front of the line, I

110

handed the golden tickets to the gatekeeper who tried to swipe them through. I was expecting to hear the pleasant sound of an electronic beep signifying all was good. Instead, all we heard was the buzz of rejection. The gatekeeper tried again, but to no avail. "Sir, your tickets appear not to be valid. You need to go back and purchase valid tickets."

I was in disbelief. I wanted to react with frustration and anger. Fortunately, I curbed that itch, and simply said, "Well sir, that can't be. I just purchased these tickets 20 minutes earlier with my Discover card." I then pulled out a piece of paper in my pocket and handed it to him. "Here's the receipt."

He glanced at it and then replied. "Oh. Well, unfortunately I can't let you into the park sir, but they should be able to take care of you over in guest services." He pointed to a building just off the path where we stood. "Just take these tickets, your receipt, and your family there."

I acknowledged him, corralled my family, and led them over to guest services. Unfortunately, the line inside the building wasn't as short as we had hoped. It was long. I looked over at my wife, and family, who were standing off to the side. I could still see in them some of the excitement of the day they had been waiting for, but it was waning. Excitement can easily turn into impatience when you have to wait.

Everything is Going to Be Okay

The people in line with me were growing impatient too. They just couldn't believe their plight. I found myself wanting to jump in and share in their misery. I wanted to commiserate with them. But I stopped myself. I knew it was going to be a long day and I wanted to make the most of what we had no matter what the circumstance.

Then I looked ahead, past the front of the line. There on the other side of the counter were Disney cast members working hard for the guests. They were calm. Despite all the frustration from those in the line, they were maintaining a positive attitude, and appeared to be genuinely trying to help everyone. I wanted to honor that. I wanted my attitude to match, if not for myself, for my family.

I simply then said to myself, "Everything is going to be okay. I can either make this a long miserable day, complaining that this is a travesty, *or* I can just keep my cool. Be patient. Be kind. Because that's what I'd want from others." That decision would impact my family and me for the rest of the day!

Grand Marshals

Once I finally got up to the Disney cast member, I smiled and explained my predicament. Their staff went right to work trying to resolve the issue. It took a while, I won't lie, but they were very kind, worked hard, and kept me informed of what they were doing. Finally, the problem was resolved. The tickets were golden again!

The Disney cast member across the counter said, "Listen, I know you've been in line a long time. I want to give you a Fast Pass so that you and your party can jump to the front of the line for up to ten rides. It's the least we can do for the time you've lost in this line today." He then handed me a Fast Pass card. I was extremely grateful and thanked him. I looked over at my family, smiled, and gave them a thumbs-up. Noticing my family of four, he then said, "You know, I'm also about to go out in the park and recruit a family to be our grand marshals today for our big parade. You've been extremely patient. Would you and your family like to be our grand marshals today? We'd be honored to have you!"

I looked back at my family, summoned my wife, and shared the request with her. The answer was easy. "Yes!" That day in February—despite the lines and the crowds—my family and I enjoyed one the greatest experiences you can imagine. The difference maker was the attitude I chose to have and which my family mirrored. However, it could have gone the other way.

My default reaction with the delays and setbacks would have been to display displeasure, frustration, and a victim-like attitude. However, I learned something that day. By simply deciding to keep my cool, be patient, and persevere with hope, I changed the wind in the sails. My attitude became a difference maker.

Attitude can turn a trying day into a pleasant day. However, if you are not careful, a slip in your attitude can turn a trying day into a very bad day. If attitude is a string on a guitar, it's you who plays the string on this. No one else does. Play it well and it can turn any good day into an even better day. When it seems that the great moments you hoped for might have been robbed, when adversity strikes, consider the possibility that even greater moments may still be on the other side of the challenge. The trick is to keep your cool and persevere.

Thomas Jefferson said it best, "Nothing can stop the man with the right mental attitude from achieving his goal; nothing on earth can help the man with the wrong mental attitude." My family and I learned this first hand. We discovered that the Disney experience— or any experience—is really what you make of it. The same is true for business. Remember your attitude sets the tone for you and your team. Your attitude influences your culture and, almost like a Jedi mind trick, it can empower the decisions made by your customers and clients in mutual favor. Attitude really is the difference maker.

Remember hope, love, and determination make for great emotions. This practical advice is what sets the right mental attitude for you to anticipate great moments.

Habit 2 - Choose Your Conduct

The great thing about attitude is that it's your choice. Nobody else chooses it for you. You decide and, therefore, create your attitude. In other words, you get to choose your response ahead of time to whatever might come your way—good, bad, or indifferent.

The significance of that is your attitude affects the outcome. One of my mentors, Scott Fay, shares that your "attitude directly determines the results you get." [40]

Every person should identify ahead of time the attitude needed to lead themselves and influence others. The right attitude is what helps create and sustain momentum. The key is to know what attitudes you value most.

The Five Leadership Attitudes

There are five significant attitudes that we can choose to value ahead of time that will affect how we lead ourselves and lead others.

1) An Attitude of Appreciation

2) An Attitude of Calm

3) An Attitude of Trust

4) An Attitude of Optimism (or Hope)

5) An Attitude of Responsibility

This list of leadership attitudes is life giving. The easy way to remember them is to recognize that the first letter of each of the keywords forms an acrostic that spells the word ACTOR.

ACTOR is a significant word because it is one of the earliest forms used to describe a leader. In Latin, the first syllable comes from the prefix "Ag" or "Act"—a verb that means "to do." The later part, the suffix, "Tor," refers to an agent of the preceding verb. In this case, an actor is an "agent of doing." But even more significant is that it has roots to the Ancient Greeks who used the word ἄκτωρ (áktōr) to denote a "leader", and the prefix is from the word ἄγω (ágō), which means "lead, carry, convey, or bring." [41] How fitting is that? Today, while the use of the word actor tends to represent a person who performs in a theatrical play or movie, its original meaning was used to identify a leader as someone who essentially leads, carries, conveys and brings influence to others.

How about that? You are an actor. How will you lead? How will you carry, convey and bring influence to others—and to yourself? Rodney Dangerfield once shared, "Acting deals with very delicate emotions. It is not putting up a mask. Each time an actor acts (or leads) he does not hide; he exposes himself." We play a significant role in influencing others. Every actor, or leader, needs to know their character. When your character is right, which is reflected by your attitude, then it's easier to be an agent of influence that can help unlock the stories of others—including yours. As an agent of influence you play a leading role; therefore, choose the right attitude. The right attitude is life giving.

Attitude is More Powerful than Fear

Chapter 3 identified twelve types of fears that we might experience at any time. Fear that can dissuade us from pressing on.

If you couple any one of these fears with the wrong attitude, it can keep you from persevering. As a recap, here are the twelve common fears.

1) The Fear of Adversity

2) The Fear of Conflict

3) The Fear of Change

4) The Fear of the Process

5) The Fear of Rejection

6) The Fear of Vulnerability

7) The Fear of Being Alone

8) The Fear of Pain (or Injury)

9) The Fear of Failure

10) The Fear of Disappointment

11) The Fear of Success

12) The Fear of Death

I don't know any leader that can't relate to more than one of these fears. When any one of these fears pays a visit, it has a tendency to produce an unhealthy attitude in us.

The Five Fatal Attitudes

Scott Hamilton, a former Olympic gold medalist and brain tumor survivor, once commented, "The only disability in life is a bad attitude." How often has a bad attitude crippled someone you know? At least temporarily? Unfortunately, many of us have been trained over the years to react to fear in a defensive, or with a duck-and-cover, mentality. We might respond to fear with one of five fatal attitudes.

1) Criticalness instead of Appreciation

2) Agitation instead of Calmness

3) Doubt instead of Trust

4) Helplessness instead of Optimism (or Hope)

5) Indifference instead of Responsibility

These are fatal attitudes because they can cause you to feel helpless and, if unchecked, can keep you and your team from moving forward.

It's not a coincidence that these five fatal attitudes are in opposition to the five leadership attitudes named earlier.

- Rather than having appreciation and thankfulness for what we have, the fatal attitude we might show is criticalness in our circumstances and ungratefulness when there is fear around us.

- Rather than having calmness when chaos and confusion is in the air, the fatal attitude we might show is agitation and frustration to those around us.

- Rather than being trusting of others, of the plan, and in our faith, the fatal attitude we might show is doubt when fear comes howling into our lives.

- Rather than finding optimism or hope, our fatal attitude might be that we choose helplessness, defeat, or resignation when a fear and doubt comes upon us.

- Rather than having responsibility for what it is that we need to do and empathy for others, the fatal attitude we might demonstrate is indifference, a lack of concern, or maybe even frustration towards others when fear is pressing down on us.

Remember that attitude is more powerful than fear. It's not fear that limits us; it's the attitude we choose in the face of fear. The right attitude, a leadership attitude, can lead us past the fear and towards our mission. It's an enabler; whereas the wrong attitude, a fatal attitude, will keep us from persevering and leading. Our attitude feeds or starves our fears. Choose the right attitude and you can face the fear.

The Emotion of Fear

Take a moment to think about a time where you experienced fear, anxiety, or frustration. Can you think of a shift in your attitude that you chose in response to the fear you felt? Even if it was an attitude you aren't proud to admit to, ultimately, you chose it, right?

Think about this further. Each of us has a choice of which attitude we display no matter what we face. The attitude we choose will help us or hurt us. It can also help or hurt the team we lead or those that we communicate to.

For example, consider a time when you faced a "fear of adversity," a "fear of change," or a "fear of the process." Perhaps your team presented an opportunity to you but, because you had that twinge of fear—the "fear of adversity," the "fear of change," or the "fear of the process"—you reacted with a fatal attitude such as indifference or unwillingness that was sensed by your team. Maybe you didn't think of it as fatal at the time, but what if that attitude lingered in the mind of your team afterwards.

In most environments—at work, home, in the classroom, or on the playing field—the attitude of the leader is commonly remembered consciously and subconsciously. It's not what is said, it's how people felt when you said it. We see this impact from coaches, teachers, customers, and supervisors. Any time a fatal attitude is received, those who witnessed it instinctively want to do their best to avoid experiencing it again in the future. That's because a fatal attitude can also produce fear in others.

As I said earlier, our attitude either fuels fear or starves it. For example, suppose the next time a new opportunity with some risk arises, a team might be reluctant to share it with the leader based on their past experience with the leader's attitude. They might fear the rejection or disappointment again, especially if the memory of a past experience, where they witnessed an attitude of indifference or unwillingness, is still fresh or a common pattern. Because of their fear, they will likely also choose the fatal attitude of unwillingness even though the opportunity might have great potential.

Isn't it interesting that any time we experience a fatal attitude it might resurface in others? Attitude feeds attitude.

So, what if the next time we face a fear we chose a leadership attitude instead of a fatal attitude? A leadership attitude can help mitigate our fears, and even turn the fears into the springboard we need to gain a sense of urgency and perseverance.

Years ago, I had a paper published at a conference and was asked to present it. I practiced in front of the mirror over and over. The fear that I felt encompassed about four of the twelve fears.

1) I was afraid of failure; I didn't want to mess up.

2) I was afraid of disappointment; I didn't want to share something not fulfilling the expectations of the audience.

3) I was afraid of rejection; I didn't want to be ridiculed and criticized at the end of the presentation.

4) And I was afraid of vulnerability; I didn't want to find out that I was not as good as I hoped I would be. I feared the exposure.

For multiple days, I practiced. Finally, the day came. I sat in the chair in the conference room a half hour before it was my turn. I pretended to be listening to the speaker before me, but my mind was on my presentation. As the minutes got closer, my heart started pounding. I thought my heart was going to jump out of my chest. I could feel the sweat on my forehead. When the facilitator called my name, I could hardly breathe. I stood up and walked to the lectern. As I looked at the audience, my heart was beating hard. I thought my voice was going to shake. But then something happened.

With the fears very real to me—failure, disappointment, rejection, vulnerability, and now death (I thought I was going to have a heart attack!)—they caused a trigger. I found myself putting on an *"attitude of optimism"*—also known as hope, which I had learned all those years before. As I put my hands on the lectern and leaned in, I also put on the *"attitude of appreciation."* I was glad to be there. I thought, *"What a great place to be and what an honor it is to share."* This attitude gave me the words I needed to start.

"Good morning! I am thankful to be here today to share my experiences with you."

I hadn't practiced that opening before. But hearing it gave me confidence, and with that statement I was able to put on the *"attitude of responsibility."* I realized they came to hear something, and I believed I had what they needed. It was my responsibility to share what I knew, no one else's.

Those three attitudes—optimism, appreciation, and responsibility—ironically were triggered because of five fears: the fear of failure, the fear of disappointment, the fear of rejection, the fear of vulnerability, and the fear of death. Taking action in response to fear with the right attitude was all I needed to present the material the best way I knew how. Coupling the right attitudes with my fears reignited my energy and helped me overcome my trepidation.

Put Fear in the Rear

Truth be told, fear can actually be one of your greatest teachers. It begs the question *why*. Why do you feel the way you feel? It's okay to let fear challenge you as long as you challenge fear right back! Fear wants to protect you, but ask it *why*.

Fear may be revealing a belief system that you have that might be wrong. What you don't want is to let fear paralyze you. Anytime fear paralyzes you it might be because you have some preconceptions that are out of alignment. Don't ignore the fear instead explore the fear. Find out *why*.

Next time you feel fear, ask yourself these questions:

- What fear is stopping me?
- Does the fear really know what's best for me?
- What is the attitude I need for my team and myself?
- How will I respond?

The short minute you take to answer these questions can totally change your perspective and your circumstances.

Wrap Up

Attitude matters. Attitude is like a rudder on a boat, it directs you on a path either towards safe traveling waters and your destination, or not used properly, it can lead you into unsafe troubled waters and disaster. When you see the squall coming in the distance, your attitude defines your approach to how you ride out the ensuing storm. The storms will come, but look for the good. The right attitude will lead you to the right options. Remember the five leadership attitudes:

- Appreciation
- Calmness
- Trust
- Optimism
- Responsibility

Your attitude as a leader is often mirrored by those you lead alongside, and by those who follow you. How are you going to act? And how are those around you going to respond? Let these five attitudes be your default state of mind. Act on them. Be an agent of influence. In this way you can manage the emotions that you and your team might feel. And you will learn how to minimize the fears. With the right attitude, your fears won't need to stop you.

The bottom line is this: to seize the good you need to put on the right attitude no matter what the circumstance. This simple choice can be the difference maker in helping you and your team press on!

Chapter 8 -
Call on Courage

The brave man is not the man with ice water in his veins; he is, rather, the one who's afraid, but still does the job.

Capt. Eugene "Red" McDaniel (former POW)

Early in our development, courage was infused into us by those who loved us. In an environment of trust and protection, we were encouraged to boldly stand, walk, run, jump, and eventually ride a bike. In the process of trying something new, we probably fell a few times, we may have cried and resisted, but the reward was greater than the risk. The more we were challenged, the greater our courage became.

In a similar environment, we were encouraged to read, write, paint, and make things. We saw ourselves as creative and courageous.

As it turns out, courage was almost instinctive in our early growth, and critical for our readiness. Within a short time, a reservoir of courage began to fill inside each of us. You could tap into this reservoir allowing you to try other things, like roller skating, swimming, skiing, or learning a new instrument. Trying other things—new things—even though we may not have been any good at it at first, gave us momentum to try other new things.

Unfortunately, over time, many stop tapping into that reservoir of courage. We grow complacent and begin to compare ourselves with others who we think are more creative. As a result, the reservoir goes dry and our potential is not fully realized.

Yet, those that learn to call on courage are the ones that find their reservoir filled. They are the ones that stay creative and pursue their dreams. It isn't that they are more talented; it's just that they are willing to take on the risk to build a business or try their hand at creating a disruptive innovation. These difference makers challenge the status quo and discover their true potential. They make an impact because they have chosen to do something courageous. They have decided to get out of the box and create their future. They are leaders.

All told there are three practices that can revitalize courage and create momentum. Keep in mind these practices are what are done in the real world, not in an isolated, safe corner of the box.

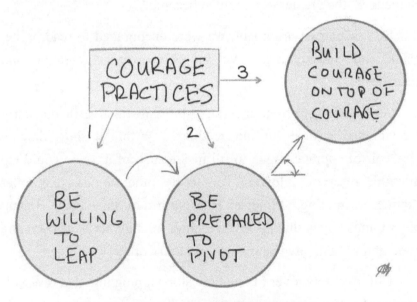

Figure 12 - Courage Practices

Practice 1 - Be Willing to Leap

On October 14, 2012, millions tuned in to their TV sets to watch an extraordinary event take place. In a hot air capsule, approximately the size of Volkswagen Bug, Austrian skydiver Felix Baumgartner, ascended to an altitude of 128,000 feet, 24 miles above the earth's surface. He was perched just on the edge of the earth's stratosphere, peering down at the globe below, waiting for the precise moment to leap from the plane.

Over 7.1 million viewers on YouTube's live stream watched in anticipation of this historic event. One follower tweeted what many felt, "Unbelievable guts to take this jump!"

Another tweeted, "This is as epic as landing on the moon."

The jump was wildly successful—captivating actually. Many who didn't watch it live tuned into the replays found on the web. Live or replay, the emotional response from leap to landing could be summarized by a simple three-letter word: Wow!

The Reason

The question for us is still, *why.* Why did he do it? Was it because he really wanted to break a record? Was it because he wanted to make history? Those potential reasons drew in the media, the viewers, and the gawkers. But what was his internal *why.*

Could it be simply that he wanted to see if he could? Men and women like Baumgartner are drawn to see if they have what it takes to do something extraordinary, something outside the box. The reality is that you and I likely have the same desire. It's not about the fame and fanfare; it's about the fulfillment of our potential. We want to prove that we can!

There were a number of times Baumgartner could simply have acquiesced to the fear, the doubt, the phobia, and the work required. He could have easily pushed the challenge away. Even at the last minute, at an altitude of 128,000 feet, he could have waved off the jump, and taken the balloon ride home.

So, what was the one thing that made him say, "Yes, I can; yes, I will?" This question is critical, because knowing the answer could change everything for you and me!

Do you dare to take a guess?

It's rather simple really. The answer is that his mission, which is "a passion for expanding boundaries," is wired with courage. [42]

The Rationale

When your mission has courage baked right in, there's a good chance you'll find a way to persevere. It doesn't mean you won't face apprehension or fear. Baumgartner had plenty of fear during his training and on that world record day—especially with his space suite.[43] However, because of his vision, he had resolved to see if he had the courage to do it and prove it. Courage is not as elusive as you might think. You don't know how much courage you have until you try.

The first practice to call on courage is to be willing to leap. If you bake courage into the endeavor, you are more likely to do it. Therefore, look at every challenge as a step of courage.

Practice 2 - Be Prepared to Pivot

The second practice to perseverance that yields courage is to be prepared to pivot. These next stories are short, but profound. They are two great examples of businesses that found courage from within in order to totally reinvent themselves and learn to pivot. Many of the great stories of perseverance are results of pivots in the midst of a crisis.

Lucky Gold

In the '70s and '80s, the discount stores offered shelf space for inexpensive electronics. A Korean electronics company known as GoldStar Electronics chose to grab the shelf space with attractively priced items such as tape players, clock radios, and even TV's. GoldStar had been in business since 1958 and was now penetrating the Western market. Their hope was to gain a significant share of the market with quality, value-priced goods that undercut the likes of Sony, Panasonic, JVC, and General Electric. But the feedback from consumers was disappointing. GoldStar become the epitome of the cliché' "you get what you pay for."

By the mid '90s it became almost impossible to find a GoldStar electronic component even if you wanted one. The shelves of the discount stores and big box stores were simply devoid of GoldStar products.

Few complained or noticed their absence. From all appearances, GoldStar seemed to have disappeared into the sunset. It was now time for new products and other brands.

But what few realize is that the Goldstar leadership recognized their short falls. They knew the world's impression of their products was poor, and that this opened the door for someone else to take over the shelves that they once occupied. However, rather than giving up, they decided to pivot. They decided that their products would be the "new brand" to fill the shelves. As a result, they reframed their mission, realigned their vision, and rebranded their company.

Today, few realize that LG—a recognized world leader in electronic goods—was once GoldStar Electronics.

In the Western market today, LG is considered one of the top providers of mobile phones, televisions, appliances, and other electronics for consumers. They are currently the 2nd largest provider of televisions, employing over 83,000 people worldwide. In 2013 alone, they generated over $53 billion dollars in global sales, and they continually push out new and innovative products every quarter.

What LG has been able to accomplish since their pivot in the mid '90s has been remarkable. It is truly a story of a business calling on courage from within to try something bold, brash and brilliant. Few could have guessed the turn around that would ensue over the next 20 years. In fact, few consumers know about the rebranding at all. To many, Goldstar is long forgotten, a different company.

Along the way, LG has acquired Zenith televisions, and have stood toe-to-toe with the likes of Samsung, Apple and Sony both in quality and in quantity of sales. Today LG stands as one of the best examples of a business that has gathered new momentum and learned to press on.

Intel

In the late '70s and early '80s, Intel was focused on manufacturing memory chips. In the early days, their business was a great success; but the competition for memory started getting crowded and Japan was simply able to produce memory chips faster and cheaper.

Intel found it exceedingly more difficult to compete in that market. Intel's president, Andy Grove, and Intel's chairman and CEO, Gordon Moore, were at a crossroads. They knew if they didn't do anything, Intel would likely die a slow death.

The one division of their business that was doing well was the newly formed microprocessor division. What had started off as a sidebar project was growing. But what had been their bread and butter—their memory business—was now falling short on sales quarter after quarter. Their business was bleeding.

They agonized over what to do. So much had been invested in the manufacturing of memory. That was their identity. It seemed ludicrous to give it up. But then they asked themselves a question. Suppose the board brought on a new president and CEO to run this company. If a new leadership team walked through that door to take our positions, what would they do?

Without batting an eye, both men instinctively knew what would happen. Because the new leadership wouldn't have as much of an emotional connection to the past, and they would close the memory division and focus entirely on microprocessors. Then Groves suggested that they pretend to be that new president and CEO and make that happen. "Why not do it ourselves?"[44]

The rest, as they say, is history. The result of that one act of courage is what turned Intel into the premier provider of microprocessors for the world. It only happened because an existing leadership team called on courage to make tough decisions for the benefit of the company.

Practice 3 – Build Courage on Courage

One thing that made the difference and allowed businesses like LG and Intel, and individuals like Felix Baumgartner, the Wright Brothers, or even you and me to achieve what might seem impossible, is our ability to call on courage. Each of us, to survive, begins to develop a courage reservoir early in life.

Courage is a component of momentum. And courage is something that creates more courage when it's put to use. In other words, courage feeds courage. Each step of courage builds more courage in you. It's quite remarkable.

If you do what you are afraid to do, then the next time it's easier. That's because you have more courage than you did before. Courage is never wasted if it's used. The key is to use it!

Decide without Emotion

A secret to leveraging courage is to try not to make decisions from an emotional state. Andy Grove shares that, "People who have no emotional stake in a decision can see what needs to be done sooner."[45] This is part of the strategy you need to consider when you call on courage. Try to separate yourself emotionally.

To help you with this, think back to when you first learned to ride a bike? Were you afraid? Sure you were. But somehow, you eventually ignored the emotional disruption for a moment and still called on courage. You took the necessary risk to do something that you couldn't do before! That act of courage built momentum for you to try other things.

You may not remember this, but prior to learning to ride a bike, you drew on courage to learn how to stand, and then to walk, and then to run. It didn't matter how many times you fell, you kept drawing on courage until you had a breakthrough. You didn't let the emotional attachment you had in the comfort of the box keep you from calling on courage.

Fast forward to the present. We can probably list all sorts of reasons why we can't, why we won't, and why we shouldn't. Our excuses can keep us from stepping out of the box of ordinary to do something new and something extraordinary. Over time, we grow stale, complacent, and, dare I say, comfortable. Many prefer the box to the candle that's lit, and that's why few achieve their potential.

Don't Suppress Your Desire for Significance

Most individuals start off feeling like that they were made for something more—something greater. Starting at an early age, a desire was born inside each of us to one day make an impact. However, over time the desire can be suppressed as the pressure to succeed begins to overwhelm, or the opportunities to pursue success seem unavailable. When this happens, the courage that was once inside of us seems to go missing.

Have you ever wondered, *where is my courage?* If that's you, there's good news. The reservoir of courage that was developed inside of you early in life is likely still there. You can learn to call on courage again any time. The key is to take the first step. Take the leap of faith. Don't suppress the desire that inside of you. The fear and feelings may try to stop you, but faith and action that builds off desire and hope can push through any fear.

Wrap Up

To call on courage, it takes practice: 1) you need to be willing to leap with faith; 2) you need to be prepared to pivot with confidence; and 3) you need to be eager to build courage on top of courage. Faith is a critical component to courage needed to help you create the future. Courage and faith are brothers. It nearly impossible to have courage without faith, and faith without courage. Courage also requires hope and trust. As for faith, it is void without courage. That's because faith without courage is like an ocean without water. Courage fills you and your team and, when the leadership of an organization chooses to call on courage, it provides the fuel needed to press on.

Phase Three -
Explore the Opportunities

Exploration is really the essence of the human spirit.

Frank Borman (Astronaut)

Most individuals want to start exploring right away. They want to get going! Hopefully you've taken time first to imagine and create. Those first two steps are critical for any leader who wants to be known as a person who perseveres. To define the path, you need to imagine and create. Now comes the next phase—the exploration phase.

According to Frank Borman, who was the first astronaut to fly around the moon, "Exploration is really the essence of the human spirit." Exploration is about going through the doors that now exist because of what you and your team have imagined and created. Exploration is about seizing the opportunities.

The exploration phase can be one of the most exhilarating components to the process. Physicist Stephen Hawking, whose life in itself is an example of perseverance, reveals that, "Exploration by real people inspires us." He's right. We are drawn in by the explorers, and when we explore we begin to see with a new set of eyes. Additionally, when we follow others who explore we desire to experience and take in their views. This section reveals four choices every leader can make with their team in exploring the opportunities.

Chapter 9 -
Go Beyond Yourself

*Only those who will risk going too far can
possibly find out how far one can go.*

T.S. Elliot

There is a profound speech at the end of the movie *The Martian* as told by actor Matt Damon. Damon is playing the lead role of astronaut Mark Watney who just survived being left behind and stranded on the planet Mars. He is now back on Earth and speaking to a group of students who want to know what it takes to persevere and survive in space. Sensing what they want to know he shares the following insight.

> At some point everything is going to go south on you and you are going to say, 'This is it! This is how I am!' Now, you can either accept that, or you can get to work. That's all it is! You just begin. You do the math. You solve one problem. Then you solve the next one. And then the next. And if you solve enough problems you get to come home. [46]

He's right. To create the future, you need to go past the present and get to work. You need to go beyond yourself. For many though, the present can be a bit of a mess. It might seem impossible to get to where you want to go because life, for you, has unraveled. If that's you, if you feel stuck, know that there's still hope.

One of my favorite stories that show how to push through and go beyond yourself is the real life event of Apollo 13. This story that took place in 1970, was also depicted in the movie of the same name starring Tom Hanks, Kevin Bacon, and Bill Paxton in the mid '90s. In this classic film, we watch how Commander Jim Lovell (Hanks) and his crew learn to withstand one challenge after another and go beyond themselves. In many ways, it's a lot like the *Martian*, except it's based on a true story!

The original mission for Apollo 13 was to be just the third group of astronauts to land on the moon. Unfortunately, just a day away from their historic landing, an explosion onboard forces them to divert their mission. A rupture of a service module connecting an oxygen tank caused the explosion. It was nearly the worst thing that could happen. They were leaking oxygen, and NASA instructed them to turn off the power in some of the modules to conserve what oxygen they had left. Things looked grim.

In 1970, the world literally watched with bated breath from their rabbit-ear television sets to hear and see what the fate might be for the three-man crew. Even in Rio de Janeiro, Brazil, where I lived at the time, my family was curious and concerned. This was especially true of my dad. Jim Lovell was a classmate of my father's at the U.S. Naval Academy, both graduates of the class of 1952. My dad, along with the whole world, was anxious to see the Apollo 13 crew return safely back home. We all prayed for a miracle.

Today their story stands as a greater success than their intended goal—a third lunar landing. What they accomplished in space was miraculous. They found a way to persevere and survive despite the odds. Today NASA officially classifies the journey as a "successful failure."

I find those words ironic: *successful failure*. It is called a *failure* because they couldn't complete their mission to land on the moon. But it was deemed *successful* because of the experience garnered in rescuing the crew and getting them back home safely.

Life is full of failures, but the best ones might be successful failures. Successful failures are the ones where perseverance plays the central role. Successful failures begin to emerge when the Menace—experienced as Grief and Pain—comes full force and yet, because of perseverance, there's still a favorable outcome. Successful failures are the stories of legends and they are worth sharing!

Here's a list of just a few individuals who experienced successful failures—all of whom are legends.

- The Apollo 13 Crew
- Walt Disney
- Michael Jordan
- Oprah Winfrey

- Albert Einstein
- Thomas Edison
- The Beatles
- U2

Successful failures are great examples of perseverance because they reflect accounts of what it takes to press on despite the mess. These individuals failed to achieve an objective—at least at first— but they didn't give up. Because of that there is a positive outcome in the end. To see past the mess and go beyond yourself, it starts with awareness of three key perspectives that every leader should strive to have.

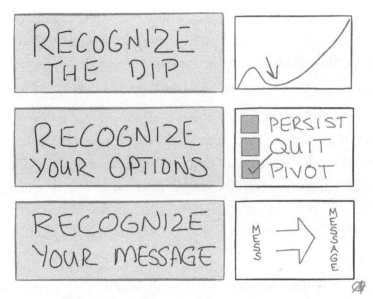

Figure 13 - Perspectives to Go Beyond

Perspective 1 - Recognize the Dip

It seems somewhere in the middle of a pursuit, something can happen that seems to jeopardize the mission or affect the journey. This unexpected resistance, or challenge, is something Seth Godin calls "The Dip." "The Dip," according to Godin, "is the long slog between starting and mastery."[47] It's best represented reflected in Figure 14.

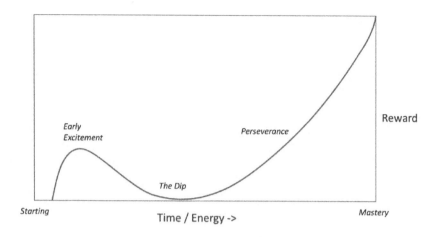

Figure 14 - Preparing For The Dip

At the beginning of the journey, there can be a lot of excitement, which in and of itself is a reward. It's satisfying. After a while, the payout of the reward and the degree of satisfaction pales in comparison to the effort required. This is when we see the first wave of challenges. This is the first sign of "The Dip." The Dip makes us want to quit. In fact, many people do.

It can take some time and energy to get through The Dip. However, the proper vision and mission – even a readjusted vision and mission, like Apollo 13, can help you push through it. Eventually, the journey will lead to a reward – it leads to mastery.

Perspective 2 - Recognize Your Options (Persist, Quit, or Pivot)

When The Dip occurs, we might question our path; we might wonder the reason. This is when life becomes messy. This is when life takes you for a loop. When this happens, and invariably it will, you need to work through what I call the "Turbulence Checklist."

If you've ever been on airplane, you have probably experienced turbulence. After the takeoff, once you are at cruising altitude, the plane might hit a rough of patch of air. The first few seconds it might not seem so bad. But after about a minute, it can get awfully uncomfortable. When this happens, the pilot has a checklist that he works through to keep everyone safe and get everyone to the appointed destination. His job is to carry out the mission as best he can.

When turbulence happens, the first item on the checklist is for the pilot to evaluate his flight options.

1) He can choose to stay on course, maintaining his altitude and airspeed, with the intent on getting to the destination as planned. But he's likely going to gather data provided by other pilots that have recently flown at that same altitude and area. He wants to know, *does the turbulence persist? How bad does it get?*

2) If the turbulence is particularly bad and expected to get worse, he can divert and land the plane at the nearest airport, opting to live to fly another day.

3) He can change altitude, airspeed and maybe even alter his direction for a bit with the intent to find a way to minimize the turbulence, yet still make progress towards the destination.

As passengers on that plane, when we first experience particularly bad turbulence, our inclination and yearning might be for the pilot to just land the plane. We want our feet back on solid ground, whereas those that fly often might be able to grin and bear it. They don't mind a little bit of turbulence. They just want to get to where they need to go, quickly. But most experienced pilots and passengers recognize the best option is to alter the altitude or path just slightly to get through the mess. It might take longer, but it turns out to be a better trip for all.

In life, when the mission seems to be in question or jeopardy, these similar options are available to you and me. When we hit "The Dip" and experience turbulence, we have three options:

a) Persist and stick with it

b) Quit and give up

c) Pivot and try a different approach

Understand your options. Should you continue? Should you quit? Or is there another way?

Option A – When to Persist

Continuing on the course you are on might seem to be the right choice, but it's not necessarily always the smart choice. Pride can make it hard to see the right path and keep us from giving up the investment of our time and our routine of how we do things. We don't want to quit, and that's noble. But, if we're doing the same thing over and over expecting a different result, then we are acting out the definition of insanity. It's easy to get burned out when repeatedly doing the same thing with no forward movement.

Instead, my advice is to be persistent about doing the little things that give you forward movement. Do the little things that can give you a sense of accomplishment and that help you focus on executing the mission. You might need to break down some of the big things you were trying to accomplish into small pieces. Even if

143

the vision is murky—sometimes just accomplishing the key things that are center point to your mission will give you the boost you need. Those are the things you want to persist in doing.

Option B – When to Quit

Quitting can be a tempting choice. Sometimes we just want to call it a day, give up, and head back to safety. However, if you quit you might always wonder. The question to ask is when is quitting the right thing to do? Is there ever an appropriate time to quit?

Surprisingly, the answer is *yes*! There are times where quitting might be the best option. The tool you use to help evaluate if quitting is the right thing to do is your mission.

Ask yourself these questions.

- What are the things I am doing right now that don't line up with my mission?

- Is there something I have committed to, or something that I am doing, that ultimately doesn't help me or my team achieve the mission or make a difference in the lives of others?

What have I said yes to that's keeping me from doing something else that would be a better use of my time or resources?

Some obvious things you might want to quit on the personal level are things like smoking, staying up late, eating junk food, or watching reruns of *Walking Dead*. But, there may be other things as well. Maybe it's your job or responsibility at work that just doesn't fit your passion, or that volunteer task that has been robbing you of doing other things. Maybe there is a relationship you are in that isn't healthy and is keeping you trapped. What about in your business?

Are you trying to do more than you ought? Every opportunity chased isn't always a good thing. Jim Collins, in his book *Good to Great*, reveals that that companies that become great don't focus solely on what to do to become great, "they focus equally on what not to do and what to stop doing."[48] His suggestion is to create a "stop doing list" and to "systematically unplug anything extraneous."

Quit what you should quit. And quit fast!

But when you do quit, make sure it's for a good reason. If quitting lets you focus and execute on more important areas of your mission, then that's a green light. Go! Free yourself up.

But if quitting gets you nowhere, then why quit? Remember, even if you quit, your end goal is still to persevere. The actions, behaviors, and tasks that you stop doing should only be eliminated if they enable you to more easily execute those other actions, behaviors, and tasks needed to press on and accomplish your mission. If the mission seems to be disrupted, what you want instead is a "successful failure" like what Jim Lovell and his crew experienced on Apollo 13. Lovell didn't quit, he just learned to pivot.

Option C – When to Pivot

The choice that great leaders make is learning how to pivot. Pivoting is about readjusting. It's about evaluating and focusing on what's essential and forgoing what's not. In some ways, pivoting requires some element of quitting—or at least changing.

The story of Apollo 13 is full of pivots. Every pivot was done to help accomplish the ultimate mission they always had—to return home safely.

When you pivot, you are reevaluating what really matters. Is there a practice or behavior that needs to be tweaked? Is there a goal within the mission that you wanted to hit that you should reevaluate or maybe jettison? Pivoting is about reorienting and eliminating waste. It's about learning how to be more effective in executing the mission and getting better clarity of the vision.

Like a pilot, you might need to change your altitude or even your direction for a while. You never want to jettison the mission, but you might need to refine it to allow more creativity to occur. Creativity is what enables you and your team to better execute.

In some ways, pivoting is similar to the flight of a Navy Tomahawk missile in pursuit of its target. For it to hit the target, the missile needs to readjust frequently or else it will miss the target entirely. Obstacles, wind, and resistance affect its flight path, but the missile reorients along the way to keep it on its flight plan and ultimately its mission.

I encourage you to review these three options. When you face a mess, do you persist, quit, or pivot?

Learn to pivot by seeing through the mess and searching for hope. Overcoming turbulence is often a matter of changing your perspective. Find hope, and then adjust to it. That gives you clarity. Recognize that the resistance you are facing isn't necessarily a cause for quitting; it's cause for pivoting and pressing on. When you train your eye to see past the mess, pivoting becomes a means to persevere.

Perspective 3 – Recognize Your Message

When you battle through the adversity and challenges, it can feel like you are in a deep mess. It's often hard to see the good that might come from Grief and Pain. But the greatest stories of hope, triumph, and inspiration, began as a mess. Some of the real world individuals who have learned to persevere by pivoting and turn their mess into a message include the likes of Louie Zamperini, Walt Disney, Michael Jordan, Oprah Winfrey, Albert Einstein, Thomas Edison, The Beatles, and U2 to name a few.

Louie Zamperini was an Olympic athlete that competed in the Berlin games, and then enlisted in the United States Army Air Corps during World War II. Unfortunately, in 1943 he and his crewmates crash-landed in the Pacific Ocean. He endured a harrowing 47 days in a bullet-shredded raft before being taken captive by the Japanese Navy. He then spent the next several years as a prisoner of war enduring brutal conditions. Reflecting on his time as a POW, Zamperini shares, "I couldn't give up hope. Not my style. I would do what I had to do to survive."[49] He did this for himself and for his fellow prisoners. His mission had a message, and because of that he learned to pivot multiple times and press on.

There are two great things about Louie Zamperini: He persevered to the end, and he maintained his mission with a positive attitude. "My persistence, perseverance, and unwillingness to accept defeat when things looked all but hopeless were the very character traits I would need to make it through World War II alive." As encouragement for you and me, he adds, "You don't have to live through a war to have those qualities work for you every day.[50]"

Walt Disney was fired from a newspaper job and told that he lacked imagination and had no original ideas. However, he ended up transforming the world with innovative films and amusement parks. His failures didn't stop him. In fact, he shared later, "I think it's important to have a good hard failure when you're young. I learned a lot out of that. Because it makes you kind of aware of what can happen to you. Because of it I've never had any fear in my whole life when we've been near collapse and all of that. I've never been afraid. I've never had the feeling I couldn't walk out and get a job doing something." Apparently, surviving failure makes you less fearful.

Michael Jordan didn't make his varsity basketball team in high school, so he played junior varsity with the intent to prove to the coach he had what it took. He once said that, "If you push me towards something that you think is a weakness, then I will turn that perceived weakness into strength." That was the message he wanted to make. After averaging 40 points a game while on the junior varsity team, it didn't take a rocket scientist to figure out he deserved to play on the varsity team the next year. Jordan knew something about the art of pivoting; it was central to his mission. His advice to you and me is to look for ways to, "Always turn a negative situation into a positive situation."

Oprah Winfrey was demoted from her job as a news anchor because she was told she wasn't fit for television. Ironically, she eventually became the most powerful and influential woman in media and has amassed a net worth of $3 billion dollars.

Thomas Edison had 10,000 failed experiments before he got the light bulb right. He might tell you, "Our greatest weakness lies in giving up. The most certain way to succeed is always to try just one more time." That was his message and his mission.

Albert Einstein wasn't able to speak as a child until he was four years old and told by his teachers he wouldn't amount to much. Today he is considered one of the greatest scientists of all time, having developed the theory of relativity.

The Beatles was an upstart band that was told they had no future in show business. Decca Records initially rejected them in 1962 stating they *"didn't like the sound. Groups of guitars were on the way out."* The Beatles, of course, became the most recognized bands of all time having seventeen songs peak at number one, and over forty songs that reached the top forty in less than a ten-year span.

The band U2, like the Beatles, were also told they didn't have what it takes at the start. In a letter written to Paul David Hewson, who is better known as Bono, RSO records told him that they felt their music was "not suitable." Not suitable? Can you imagine? U2 is the most iconic band of all time spanning both the end of the 20th century and beginning of the 21st century having sold over 170 million records. What if they had not persevered? We would have missed out on some great music. As far as RSO Records, apparently they still haven't found what they are looking for. The last great artists to its credit were the Bee Gees and Barbra Streisand.

Wrap Up

The common denominators in the great stories of success—especially successful failures—are that the leaders in the story experienced some type of dip. Despite the dip, they learned to pivot and persevere. Because of that, they were able to turn what looked to be a mess into a message. Nothing ever built that was great was done so without risk of failure. Fail fast, get back up, and try again.

Keep in mind the line from the movie *The Martian*: "You solve one problem. Then you solve the next one. And then the next. And if you solve enough problems you get to come home."

My challenge to you is this: if a mess can transition into a message, then let that be part of your mission too. Significance is knowing that you've made an impact because you've shown the world you've gone beyond yourself! And when you press on like that— when you go beyond yourself— others want to press on too.

Chapter 10 -
Take On Challenges with Passion

You've got to have an idea, or a problem, or a wrong that you want to right that you're passionate about; otherwise, you're not going to have the perseverance to stick it through.

Steve Jobs

One common thread exists in almost every story of perseverance. Those that truly lead achieve success because they battled through adversity with passion. Success—real success—doesn't come in the absence of adversity. It comes instead by a passionate pursuit in the presence of adversity. I call this *leadership passion*.

The next story I want to share is about young man named Michael, who happens to be my son. When I first wrote this story it was from a third person account. In early drafts, he was given a different name, and I never revealed that my wife and I were the parents.

For months, the story sat written in third person narrative. Eventually with Michael's permission, I inserted his name in it, but still I never revealed the parents. Again, the story sat for a while as I built the other pieces of this book. It was a central story for me, and the most impactful piece related to perseverance that I knew personally.

However, early readers of the manuscript, while they liked the story, felt it was someone else's story that I was just leveraging.

Because of that, it didn't connect the way I had intended. So I went back and reworked it, and it is now shared the way it happened. It is a first person account from the perspective of a parent—namely me. It's a story about a young man, who despite all odds, found a way to persevere and prove the naysayers wrong. He is an inspiration to me and my family, and I hope this story inspires you as well.

From his story, I discovered that anyone who is willing to push pass the doubt—especially doubt expressed by others—could learn to be an effective leader through passion. This can be accomplished by working through three stages of a challenge as illustrated in Figure 15. As challenges increase, don't lose heart, instead maintain the passion!

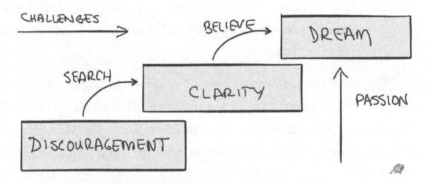

Figure 15 - Stages of a Challenge

Stage 1 – The News of Discouragement

When it comes to dealing with adversity, there is perhaps none more discouraging than a health-related one. Imagine being brought into the world proclaimed initially as a healthy baby, only to discover months later than there was a problem that happened early on—a problem that could affect you for the rest of your life.

Stroke in Utero

For us as parents, the diagnosis was, "stroke in utero." The words seemed unfathomable. For a brief moment in the neurologist office, it seemed as if time had stopped. Those words just hung in the air. The only movement in the room was the toddler in my wife's lap. And he held the gaze of all three adults in the room.

Sensing the attention, my young son, Michael, looked up and smiled. Seizing the moment, he quickly pointed toward something that caught his interest earlier. It was some blocks in the corner, and he tried desperately to scoot off my wife's lap to go investigate. He had just learned to walk a few months earlier and was the mischievous type. He loved balls, trucks, and everything else a fifteen-month-old child would love. However, his walk was different than most. He toe-walked. His left heel never struck the floor. Also, he often held up his left hand clenched and clubbed.

"What does that mean? Stroke in utero?" my wife asked. She was the first to break the silence. "And how did that happen?" she added.

With a gentle nod, our neurologist had anticipated the question. "Well, what we've found on Michael's MRI is a lesion on the right part of his brain. It shows the he possibly had a stroke at or around the time he was born, probably during labor," he paused. "It is a condition we technically call left-sided hemiplegia or hemiparesis because it affects the left side of his body physically. It can be caused during labor if there is insufficient oxygen for the baby. This causes undue stress."

Labor had been difficult. Overly long. Very stressful. But other than that it had been a normal pregnancy and Michael was brought into the world through a natural childbirth. For me, I couldn't have been more proud of my wife and the gift of our son. But something began to emerge during Michael's early development that brought us mild concern. His right leg and arm were significantly more developed and coordinated than his left side. I initially assumed he was going to be right handed and right footed. In fact, he seemed unusually strong on the right side. I thought the left side would simply catch up.

But for my wife, Barb, she knew instinctively that something was amiss. That there were some oddities that just didn't make sense to her. He only rolled in one direction on the floor, and only he walked around his crib in one direction. The left foot chose to bear as little weight as possible and relied on his toes to step and stand. But the news in that doctor's office was not what we expected.

The doctor interrupted our thoughts. I am sure we both looked dazed and confused. "Listen, your son's physical development may have been hampered by a traumatic birth, but I see no cognizant dilemmas and impediments."

All three of us looked over at Michael; he was now playing with the blocks, busy building a fort. The doctor added, "He is a very bright young boy."

I swallowed hard and looked over at my young son. What I saw just didn't add up. He looked normal. He was smart. He was happy. He just had a peculiar gait to his walk. Surely this was a temporary problem.

In my mind, I churned it over further. Michael could throw a ball across the room and chase after the dog. Sure, it wasn't fluid,

vary. You can go from frustration and anger, to feelings of guilt or sadness.

Unexpected news is the worst type of adversity possible. It is Grief and Pain in full display. Yet there are only two choices when Grief and Pain show up. You can either play the role of a victim, or rise up and march forward as victor.

It wasn't easy, but Barb and I chose to rise up and march forward. We wanted to do everything we could to help our son. By helping him, we could help ourselves.

Stage 2 – The Search for Clarity

I don't want to minimize the potency of Grief and Pain though. As parents the news was intense. It had been totally unexpected. As an engineer, I wanted to solve the problem.

"What's this all mean? Is there a surgery? Is there something we can do?" I asked the doctor.

The doctor looked up. "Well, Michael's case is mild, but unfortunately we can't go in and just fix it. The best thing for you to do is to get Michael started with occupational therapy, physical therapy, and possibly speech therapy."

Barb spoke up next. "Hmmm. What do you mean occupational therapy?" She wanted answers too. "Isn't that for adult stroke victims trying to get back into the work force? And why speech therapy?"

"Yes, but we also have some great specialists in the pediatric field," our doctor said, continuing, "I would want him to get more dexterity in his left hand and improve his fine motor skills, and that's where occupational therapy will help." He paused, "As for the speech therapy, it's just standard procedure to make sure he's right where he needs to be."

He then injected the first bit of hope since arriving. "Listen. While we can't go in there and correct the problem, we know this. The brain is an incredible organism. With the right focus and right therapist—and with your help too—his brain can learn to reroute the signals to open up his hand more easily and use it much like his right hand. The same can be said for his gait."

There was more exchange with the doctor and, eventually, many other medical professionals—many who were very helpful, but not always hopeful.

There's No Help without Hope

After that visit, we begin to search the Internet, which was new to the masses, to find out all that we could. Unfortunately, the Internet, especially in those days of dial-up, didn't present the simple solution as I had hoped for. In fact, although the Internet was very helpful, most people who post and share on the Web are those struggling, looking for help, wanting to blame someone else, and are happy to tell you their horror stories and the ones you are going to face too.

Our best source information, we felt, was to continue to find and seek out specialists.

One day we took Michael to see a highly recommended professional. However, this medical professional offered some profound words that almost resulted in instant defeat.

"May I be straight forward with you?" he asked us.

"Of course!" we responded.

"I know you want your child to grow up and do all the other things other kids do that are his age. But don't expect him to learn to ride a bike, or skateboard, roller skate, or much less play soccer with other kids his age."

I was astonished. "What do you mean?" I asked.

"Well, your son is simply not going to be able to do what other kids can do physically at the same level. And I think it's best for you, as parents, to be aware of that so you two don't have false expectations."

We were dumbfounded. Confused.

And then he added, "You want to limit the potential disappointments."

Those words I know he offered were with great intention, but the real payload of the message was packed with limiting beliefs. They were crippling. The real impact of his statement was to keep our son from living to his potential; to keep Michael from living out the adventures and dreams any young boy might have.

The message sounded like this to me. "Hey, this is a very real impediment. And you don't want to mess with the challenges that are coming for Michael. The challenges—if you face them—will discourage you and defeat him. Instead, run for cover, get Michael to a spot where he doesn't have to face any undue adversity. Keep him safe from potential harm and embarrassment. Keep him in the box."

If a message isn't hopeful, it isn't helpful.

Like kryptonite, a message void of hope, well intended or not, can zap you of your strength and resolve. Leave you barely alive. For me, this professional's message was defeating—at least initially. When there is no hope, there is no vision.

An Antidote to Limiting Beliefs

Fortunately, my wife Barbara chose to challenge the limiting beliefs. She chose to seek out hope for our son rather than run from the adversity. If we were going to go forward with life, then she believed we had to face adversity head on—including the limiting beliefs.

We soon found that every ounce of hope discovered could be something to be shared. When you share hope it multiplies; it grows wings.

One other person who knows what it's like to have a physical impediment and make something of it is Nick Vujicic, who I had a chance to meet with a few years ago.

Nick was born without legs or arms. No limbs. Like Michael, he faced some major hurdles in life—only bigger! Today, Nick stands tall on a platform of hope. He is one of the most inspiring people I have met. Nick shares these thoughts on the subject of hope.

"[Hope] is where dreams begin. It is the voice of your purpose. It speaks to you and reassures you that whatever happens to you doesn't live within you." [51]

Nick has captured something profound here. He has recognized that hope is in and of itself a belief. And hope is the one belief that has no limit. It's the one belief that can overcome the other beliefs that limit us.

159

Nick adds that, "Hope is a catalyst. It can even move obstacles that seem immovable." [52]

He is spot on. Hope is indeed a catalyst. And Barb's discipline in helping Michael—or me, for that matter—has always been paired with hope. Hope is a catalyst that breeds clarity. And perseverance is measured by seeing hope in action. Seeing hope in action is all about dedication and discipline.

A result of commitment and enthusiasm is that the limiting beliefs began to shatter. Michael eventually learned to do all the things he was told he might not be able to do. Ride a bike. Skateboard. Roller skate. Mountain climb. Play varsity soccer in high school. And he did all of these things at the same rate and at the same age as his friends and peers. Nothing slowed him down.

I sometimes go back and think what if Barb and I had not challenged the limiting beliefs? What if we had submitted to Grief and Pain and settled for less, instead of facing adversity head on?

Imagine the opportunities missed; a life not fully lived. If there's no risk, there's no reward. If there's no risk, hope dies on the vine. But perseverance requires risk. It's the antidote for limiting beliefs.

Stage 3 – The Pursuit of a Dream

One of Michael's most triumphant moments occurred in the eighth grade. At this point, Michael had gone through exhaustive physical therapy, he had worn multiple foot braces, he had multiple Botox injections to relax his muscles, and he had an extensive surgery at Shriner's Hospital in Philadelphia to stretch his heel cord. Life had not been easy. But he was determined.

One thing Michael wanted to learn how to do was play guitar. His first attempt at it a few years earlier was not easy. His guitar teacher felt that his left hand just couldn't hold the guitar and work the chords. So he restrung the guitar so that he could strum with his left and play the chords with his right. But, still Michael wasn't quite getting it.

Encouraged to try something different, Michael decided to try playing drums. Soon our house was filled with the constant battle rhythm and drive of the snare and bass drum. Slowly, the beat went from chaotic to a lively, enjoyable rhythm. It brought life to Michael and also to the rest of us.

Having mastered the drums, he then proclaimed his desire to again try to play the guitar. He had perfect clarity of what he wanted to do, and had proven with his play of the drums he had the discipline to learn how to do it.

We never wanted to refuse his desire to learn and try, so we helped him buy a newer guitar. Michael went after learning with a vengeance. This time without the strings reversed. Chords would be played on the left. The strings to strum would be on the right.

Because he had conquered the drums, momentum was on his side. Over a short period of time, he found a way for his left hand to grip the guitar and finger all the chords. His dominant right hand simply assisted his left hand with perfect strumming and added rhythm to his play.

Talent Show

Soon after learning guitar, Michael proclaimed a desire to enter the eighth grade talent show. As parents, I admit we were nervous.

Scared to death for him. He was nervous, too, but wanted to do it. We heard him practice—and practice and practice. We knew he was capable of performing well. So, scared or not, we encouraged him to go for it—and he wanted to do it by himself.

I asked him, "What do you mean, by yourself?"

"Well I need to do this without your help. Dad, if I see you and Mom there, you will make me even more nervous. Let *me* do this!"

He then made me promise not to sneak in later that day to watch. To just pray for him.

I was on pins and needles all day. I honored him by not showing up. The rest of this account is from the testimonies of others— teacher, staff, students, and parents who were there, and from Michael. I only wish I had snuck in to watch for myself.

The talent show was around lunchtime. The nerves were high, but so was Michael's excitement. After a few other students went, Michael's name was called. It seemed that the whole school was in disbelief when they heard Michael's name summoned to the stage.

"What? Michael is going to play guitar?"

Many of them didn't know he played. He was well liked, but had been shy about sharing his love for guitar. Michael walked up to the stage, plugged in his guitar to the amp coolly and calmly. He didn't say anything. And just began to play with focus and a building intensity.

Teachers, students, and staff waited with baited breath. Their expectations, they admit, were not very high. They only hoped it wasn't going to be too loud, wasn't too offbeat, wasn't going to be too scratchy.

Michael started slow. Working on just a few strings. Building a simple rhythm. A simple pattern. Then he added new elements to the play. He grew more confident. People in the room begin to take notice. It didn't sound too bad. They were pleasantly surprised.

Along with the strum of the chords, there was a melody he began to pick out and play, adding to the mix. It became more intricate. More complex. More beautiful.

Soon the rhythm began to grab the teachers' and students' attention. Everyone in the room began experiencing something powerful. Something amazing. Something unexpected.

The music continued to build and then closed with such energy that the room full of students and teachers erupted and cheered. They had been emotionally taken on a trip from bewilderment, wonderment, and impossibility to satisfaction, joy, and triumph.

Years later some of those teachers, parents, and former students occasionally reminisce with me about the moment. They remember Michael in eight grade—at that talent show.

"I just couldn't believe it. I never saw it coming."

"Michael blew everyone away!"

"That was something special."

I am always grateful for those words. The lesson for me is that the limiting beliefs we might have, which others may have impressed upon us, are meant to be shattered. The only way to shatter a limiting belief is to pursue and persevere what seemingly is impossible. It starts with clarity of what you hope for and the drive and discipline to prove it's possible. For me, I find both my sons an inspiration. And in this regard, Michael has proven to me time and time again that we shouldn't allow limiting beliefs (our own or others) to be imposed by the adversity and challenges that we might face. On the contrary, adversity and challenge is simply one more reason to try. Success really is the sum of small efforts repeated day in and day out.[53]

Engineering Degree

Today, Michael is in his early twenties. He still plays guitar, but he has also pursued another dream—his dream to be an engineer. This has not been an easy journey either. When he was a freshman in high school, we were encouraged by the school staff "to lower the bar" of his expectations. That his engineering vision would be virtually too difficult to master. The school counselor gave Michael every reason why he couldn't and shouldn't do it. But Michael, as only he could do, gave himself every reason why he could and would.

With clarity and desire, Michael focused and worked hard those four years of high school to prove his counselor wrong. By his senior year, he was taking AP Calculus and AP Physics. The following year after graduation, he enrolled in a small university in Nashville majoring in electrical engineering and did quite well. A year later, he transferred to Virginia Tech.

Then, before I knew it, which was just four years after high school graduation, he walked with his college classmates and received his diploma with a BS in electrical engineering. As I watched him walk up to the stage, my mind went back to an encounter I had when he was with me at bike shop almost 18 years earlier.

I was looking at bikes, and Michael was tagging along with me. He was about four. An older gentleman who was also looking at bikes took particular interest in Michael and then came up to me.

"Excuse me, I couldn't help but notice your son's gait and that he is a toe walker."

At first I was taken back. I wondered, why would some come up and be so forward about my son.

He continued, "I'm sorry. I should have introduced myself. My name Dr. Anderson and I am a pediatrician in town. I just want you to know that in my thirty-plus years of practice I've had the privilege to treat children with similar conditions as I noticed with your son." He then asked me a few questions about Michael, including what he enjoyed and what we had done to help him. After I shared just a little bit with him, he then put his hand on my shoulder. "I want you to know that there's hope. There are lots of things they can do now. And I have personally seen children with conditions much like your son—maybe worse—who work through it and do extremely well."

He went on, "Let me tell you, there's nothing more satisfying than to one day see them on their day of graduation walk up to receive their diploma without ever noticing the limp." He then added, "Don't ever think that your son can't do it—because one day he will!"

I still remember that conversation so vividly. Fast-forward eighteen years later to Blacksburg, Virginia. It's graduation day at Virginia Tech. A day where those good doctor's words proved to be prophetic.

In an auditorium filled with graduates and their families and friends, you would have easily found me, my wife Barbara, and my but I thought that as he would develop, the gait issues would just go away.

The doctor once again interrupted my thoughts. "His hemiparesis is what I would classify as mild cerebral palsy, which only affects him physically."

"What? Cerebral palsy? Did I hear him right?" I wondered.

Cerebral Palsy

Those two words hit like a hard plank across my face. My wife and I didn't see that coming.

"Cerebral palsy? My son has cerebral palsy?" I asked.

"Well, technically, we don't like to call anything cerebral palsy. Cerebral palsy is such a big bucket label for things like this." He paused. "Others might label your son with cerebral palsy, but you won't see that on any official medical reports—at least from our office."

The doctor continued, "The lesion, which is actually on his right region of the cortex affects his gait and fine motor skills with his left hand. It affects the use of his muscles. But, as you can tell..." he paused for a moment, "As you can tell, he is quite mobile and curious, which is what you'd want for someone with this impediment." He then added, "Officially I am calling it mild left-sided hemiparesis because what we don't see are any limitations with him cognitively."

The doctor had tried to soften the blow, but when the news is unexpected as it was for my wife and me, it can still take the wind right out of you. This can be true for any of us. Whether it is health related, financially related, or business related, the emotions will youngest son Ryan proudly watching Michael walking up in procession to receive his diploma. The limp is forgotten; it's without notice. And when they called his name to receive his diploma, you would have seen one dad—me—standing to his feet and cheering his son's name at the top of his lungs. It was uncharacteristic of me, but I simply couldn't help myself. It was a vision realized!

In that moment, tears began to run down my face. I couldn't have been more proud of him.

Michael, you have proven that when someone believes enough in a vision and works hard with passion and determination—despite the doubt from others—there's always a way to press on and achieve success. I want to just take a moment in the middle of this book and thank you for being an inspiration for me, mom, and your brother!

Wrap Up

I shared the story of Michael for one simple reason: leadership is not bounded by one's title, one's degree, one's stature in a company, or one's socio-economic situation. Anybody, at any age, can lead and influence others.

Challenges will come, but every challenge is an opportunity to lead. Lead with passion. Lead with conviction. Lead with determination. Lead! And, whatever you do, don't let anyone say you can't, or say you shouldn't, or say you don't have what it takes because you do have what it takes. Recognize taking on challenges with passion is what helps you and others persevere and press on!

Chapter 11 -

Improvise. Adapt. Overcome.

If it comes to you against the situation,
don't let the situation win.

MacGyver

W hen you begin exploring the opportunities, you'll quickly find that you're never really done creating. Creating is something you must be prepared to continue to do, especially in the face of a challenge.

The Marines have a motto centered on a simple idea, *"Improvise. Adapt. Overcome."*[54] It's become an unofficial slogan that is part of the Marine Corps culture that was coined by the legendary actor Clint Eastwood in the movie *Heartbreak Ridge*. *"Improvise. Adapt. Overcome."* is a statement of preparation necessary for those who are willing and ready to persevere.

When I was a Boy Scout, we had a similar motto, "Be Prepared." It was a simple mantra backed with a genuine emphasis that our duty as scouts was to be engaged and in a state of readiness as we explored life. It served as a reminder that we must be ready to help, ready to lead, ready to pivot, and ready to make the right decisions at the right time.

"Be Prepared" doesn't mean you need to have everything lined up before you head down the path. "Be Prepared" means you are ready to adapt while you are active on the path, and you are ready for whatever may come. This type of preparation is what allows you to improvise and overcome the challenges that you might face when you are exploring

This readiness mindset is what leaders need to persevere. Great leaders, those that know how to improvise, adapt, and overcome, exhibit four key behavioral qualities as illustrated in Figure 16.

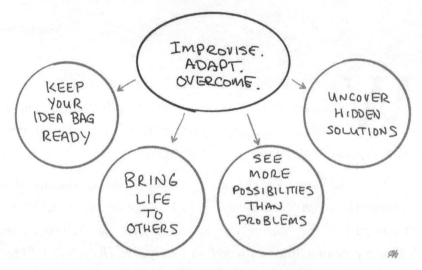

Figure 16 - The Readiness Mindset

Quality 1 - Keep Your Idea Bag Ready

MacGyver was one of my favorite TV shows to watch back in the late '80s. I tuned in every Monday night with my friends, as a sort of TV appetizer before we watched Monday Night Football. For about three years it was a ritual.

As leaders go, MacGyver is not a bad role model. Now, I'm not proposing you start carrying duct tape and a Swiss Army knife around as tools to persevere, although there may be some merit to that. But if there's one trait that we should emulate from MacGyver, it's his knack to see things differently than others in the room. That's what leaders do. They see solutions through problems.

I can remember as far back as the pilot episode. Mac is sent in to rescue a group of scientists trapped in an underground facility. As he is strategizing with the first responders before he embarks on his journey, one of the rescue experts notices Mac's near empty knapsack.

"You know it's gonna take a lot more than you can carry in that knapsack to get you through all this," he says to Mac.

Mac looks down at his knapsack and then responds with a comment that made me pause. "Well, the bag is not for what I take, it's for what I find along the way."

Sure enough, as the episode unfolds, along the journey Mac puts into the bag things that have the potential to help him persevere and succeed. Some of these items may be things that you and I would likely have never found valuable. But because Mac has a vision for success—he has defined what success looks like before he left for the journey—he is aware of how these items could possibly be used to create success. As you would expect, by the end of the episode, we see him persevere, overcoming one obstacle after another, and creatively using what he has in his bag to succeed.

After watching a rerun of the pilot episode years later, the thought hit me that the bag is a metaphor for any great leader. The bag represents the mindset of someone who may not be fully equipped at the start of a journey, but they know somehow that they will be fully resourced along the way. During the journey, these leaders who press on keep an eye out for the resources that will let help them adapt and persevere. The resources that they find along the way may vary greatly. They can range from people they may meet, the processes and systems they may come up with, or the resources they discover.

The idea bag, as a metaphor, indicates that you are ready— ready for the journey. The collection of the resources and ideas placed in your bag along the way will help you lead yourself and lead others.

Quality 2 - Bring Life to Others

There's an old adage that says, "To the world you may be one person, but to one person you may be the world." For me, and dozens of others, my uncle, Jay Kershaw, was one person who meant the world to those within his reach. He was a leader. An impact guy. An influencer.

Jay was a brilliant engineer and one of the pioneers of the computer era that helped bring shipboard computers to the sea for the Navy and other computational devices to the work environment. When I was an aspiring young engineer at twenty years old, Jay inspired me. His stories of building things based on only what had been imagined captivated me. And like MacGyver, he could engineer and build things from just about anything in the room.

He also had an incredibly positive outlook on life. His laugh could be heard across the room and would draw others in, including me. It was from him that I learned this truth. "Your outlook affects your output, and output always comes back around as input." He would clarify, "If you gain the right outlook on things then you will have the right output to get stuff done. And that comes back around as favorable input." In other words, what you sow is what you reap.

When my SimVentions partners Larry, Steve, and I started our company, Jay advised and inspired us early on. He encouraged us with his experience and insight. He grew excited hearing our progress and his passion helped shape in us a ready mindset that still exists today.

When Jay passed away in early 2014, I was asked to share some thoughts about him at his memorial service. I had plenty of stories, but I also wanted input from my family. When I asked my son what his thoughts were of Uncle Jay, a man he adored as much as I did, he thought for a moment and then simply said to me. "Dad, just the way he lived his life spoke words into me. You can share that."

I love my son's comment. It made me realize that each of us have an opportunity to live our life in such a way that we can speak life into others. We can inspire people not by *what* we do, but *how* we do it, and *why* we do it. Our *why* has to be that we care for something greater than ourselves.

Jay demonstrated this in three ways: he was curious, he was resourceful, and he was positive.

Be Curious

Jay was nosey—in a good way. You see he genuinely cared about people. When we would talk, he'd often ask me, "What's going on with the family" or "What's going on with the business?" Even at summer picnics, "What's going on with that grill that's not working?" Then with a laugh, he'd ask, "Did you forget to light the match?" He was always quick with the wit coupled with a hearty laugh. If there was a problem, well that's where his next strength shined through.

Be Resourceful

He was a problem solver, the quintessential engineer. Just like a real life MacGyver, if there were a problem, he'd design a solution. Even if you didn't think you had a problem, he'd still design you a solution.

One time my brother, Kurt, and I had trouble with the charcoal getting lit and staying lit. After witnessing the problem, Jay said, "Hold on just a second," and walked away. A minute later he came back out with a hair dryer plugged into a long extension cord. He flicked the hair dryer on, aimed it at the grill, and the coals instantly begin to flame. Ten minutes later, we were dining on delicious hot dogs. I think I was about thirteen when I saw that little trick and thought he was a genius.

One other time before, there appeared to be some rattles behind the trim of my dad's brand new 1977 Malibu station wagon. He pulled out his toolbox, unfastened all the trim work, and spent the whole day, with our help of course, rebuilding the car from the inside out. Eventually, he pulled out an empty Coke can that had been left behind the panel. It was a souvenir left by the factory workers. After the fact, we joked that the car started the day in Jay's driveway as a Chevrolet, but through his leadership in reassembling it, we turned it into a Cadillac.

Years later, when my dad's health was on the decline and with little time left on his clock, Jay stepped in and solved a big need for my family. We didn't realize that my dad's will had unfortunately lapsed, but Jay perceived the problem and brought his concern to our attention. Then, rather than just identifying the problem, he sought out a solution using the resources in his bag, namely the people he knew. Within a short period of time, he was able to track down the lawyers across the state of Colorado who would make sure all of Dad's affairs we're in order. I will forever remember that. Again, "To the world you may be one person, but to one person you may be the world."

Be Positive

Ninety-nine percent of the time, Jay was always positive and cheerful! The one exception was when I leaned on his makeshift shelf that held up his gadgets, and everything toppled over like a badly played game of Jenga (that rattled him a little bit, but not for long). Other than those rare occasions, he was always positive and cheerful. If he was down, he always found a way to get back into a positive mindset. The biggest thing I learned from Jay is that, your outlook drives your output, which feeds your input.

I encourage you to take notice of how your outlook (how you feel about what's happening) affects your output (what other people see). Then observe how quickly that output (how you are expressing how you feel) influences the input you get from others. Take notice how a simple shift in attitude—your outlook—can change your environment.

Jay's energy was infectious. A can-do attitude mixed with a hearty laugh that drew others to him. A positive outlook results in a positive output, which comes back around as positive input. Conversely, if you are negative (complaining, backbiting), others get negative; that comes back around too.

Jay is a great example of the importance of staying ready with a positive attitude. He demonstrated that we should be on the lookout for two things: things that we are thankful for and things that we might be able to help fix. This is the approach he used time and again to gain the right outlook and to persevere.

Quality 3 - See Possibilities Over Problems

Some might chalk up MacGyver as an old TV show wrapped up in make-believe. But think for a moment about your life. Don't you and I have obstacles that pile up one after another? There's nothing make-believe about that, is there? And, if you look back at your successes, weren't there things that came into your awareness that you put into your idea bag that allowed you to improvise, adapt, and overcome?

What if I told you that the type of problems that might cause other people to stumble and fall and ultimately lose heart could prompt you instead to see opportunities and solutions? Would you want that?

That is the heart of the challenge that noted author and psychologist, Dr. Kathy Cramer, revealed to me in a conversation when discussing her book, *Lead Positive*. Cramer probed further. "How much more effective would we be, and how many more could we inspire if we could condition ourselves to see more possibilities than problems?"

I was fascinated with the proposition. In her book, she proposes that leaders should "offer a compelling vision of the future by reframing problems into possibilities."

It's an interesting discussion that dives into a mindset centered on something she and her team has pioneered called Asset-Based Thinking or ABT. ABT is the mindset representative of the MacGyver mentality, a mentality she describes as turning those "what-ifs" into leadership realities. Pick up any episode of MacGyver and you can see this in play. This is ABT in action. ABT was something also I found in play for my uncle, Jay Kershaw, too. It was the way he lived his life. It became a habit for living!

So, what's the secret to making ABT a habit for living?

The secret, it turns out, is to first understand the habit loop. According to Charles Duhigg, author of the best-selling book *The Power of Habit,* we find that a habit loop is comprised of three components. [55]

1) The Cue (or trigger)

2) The Routine (or behavior)

3) The Reward (or craving)

Put all three of these things together, make it a reoccurring pattern, and you will have formed a habit. Change any one of these components, and you can change a habit.

The important habits are keystone habits, which are those habits that define who you are and are formed on a daily basis. ABT becomes a keystone habit for leaders who persevere. And the cues, routines, and rewards for those leaders and businesses with the ABT mindset are the following:

- Cue – Recognize a problem needs to be solved.

- Routine - Look for the opportunity in the problem. Collaborate with the person affected by problem. Get more clarity, if necessary. Again, keep thinking of it as an opportunity. Identify the resources around your or available to you that might offer an alternate way to go after the opportunity and solve the problem. Leverage those resources to create a solution.

- Reward - Watch the problem go away. Celebrate with satisfaction.

Those with the ABT mindset see not just the problem, but also the opportunities. Then they find the various solutions and available assets to overcome the problem. It's almost like a game.

The challenge for us to mimic this behavior is to identify the opportunity in the problem, and then work with various resources we find to develop creative solutions that overcome the problem. Also, sometimes we need just a little bit of adversity to heighten our ability to look for those things that might help us along the way.

Regarding this ready mindset, Cramer expresses that when leaders, "shift what they see, say, and do toward what is possible" they simply go further than those that don't.[56] Consider these ten leaders who were identified as the "30 Most Innovative Business Leaders of 2013"[57]

- Tim Cook (Apple)

- Angela Ahrendts (Burberry)

- Sheryl Sandberg (Facebook)

- Jørgen Vig Knudstorp (LEGO)

- Reed Hastings (Netflix)

- Mark Parker (Nike)

- Evan Spiegel (Snapchat)

- Howard Shultz (Starbucks)

- Elon Musk (Tesla Motors and SpaceX)

- Dick Costolo (Twitter)

According to Cramer, ABTers like at these leaders look at themselves and the world through the lens of "what is working, what strengths are present, and what the potentials are." Essentially, these are the "routine" or activities of a healthy habit for a person that is ready to persevere with a ready mindset. I recommend getting yourself in the right frame of mind, learning to ask these questions when facing a problem.

- What's working?

- What strengths and resources are available?

- What is the potential of using these resources to overcome obstacles in the way of progress?

Just for comparison, the corollary to ABT is Deficit-Based Thinking, or DBT. DBT, unfortunately, seems to be an all too familiar pattern in the world around us. In a conversation I had with Kathy Cramer in 2014, she shared that DBTers look at themselves and the world around them in terms of "what is not working, and what is lacking." She added, "For them it's about seeing the gaps between where they are at and where they would prefer to be."[58]

As I thought about how she described it, what came to mind for me is the character Eeyore from the classic children's story *Winnie the Pooh*. Eeyore was a DBTer, always moping, always down. One of Eeyore's sayings that I find poignant is, "I was so upset I forgot to be happy."

In life, there seem to be Eeyore's all around us, doesn't there? People that are so upset they forget to be happy. You might find them at the grocery store, gas station, workplace, or at a family reunion. They are the folks that have the habit of complaining and whining.

DBTers are often victim-like thinkers, whereas ABTers are victor-like thinkers. They are not wallowing in the loss; they are anticipating a positive outcome, even in times of difficulty.

Individuals, teams, and leaders focused solely on the issues, failures, and deficiencies may see nothing but the gaps and will often lack the vision needed to move forward. Perseverance is simply not compatible with DBTers. However, perseverance is a keystone habit for ABTers. Furthermore, what's even more impactful is that ABTers can learn to lead DBTers through adversity. DBTers, after all, are still hoping for a solution too.

Quality 4 - Unlock Hidden Solutions

Legendary soul artist, James Brown, once sang, "You got to use what you got to get just what you want." I laugh at that line, but it's true. Real success isn't in what we have; it's in what we do with what we have.

If you happen to watch the pilot episode of MacGyver—or any episode of MacGyver for that matter—you will see that by the end of the show, Mac has used all the things he collected along the way. The bag that he fills, he ends up emptying. He doesn't collect to keep something that he can later put on the mantle as a trophy. He collects to reap something that can help him carry out his mission to lead others. This is how you and I should lead too.

Wrap Up

As you gear up for this journey, I encourage you to grab your idea bag. Be ready to identify and collect some things along the way that could help you improvise, adapt, and overcome.

Next, be ready to bring life to others. We have a credo at SimVentions that represents the heart of this message, "Your Success is Our Honor." When you bring life to others—when you help them be successful—you'll find it's an honor and blessing to have that type of impact. Real success isn't in what you have; it's what you do with what you have. Perseverance has to do with using what you have to influence a better outcome for others. It's a matter of engagement.

Finally, if you prepare with an improvise, adapt and overcome mindset, you'll begin to see more possibilities than problems, and you'll recognize solutions that are right in front of you, which others might fail to see. Being ready to innovate will help you create and explore the future you have envisioned and will allow you to help others press on too.

Chapter 12 -
Stay Inspired

*I have to get inspired by something that
touches my soul, or rocks my soul.*

Steven Tyler

Exploring what inspires is another mindset choice that will help you and your team persevere. Being inspired and staying inspired increases your effectiveness four ways.

- Being inspired moves you across the starting line

- Being inspired gets the candle lit

- Being inspired motivates you to stay passionate

- Being inspired encourages others around you

The trick though is how. How does one get inspired?

In the middle of a struggle, we might find ourselves in desperation. Desperation is something none of us want; yet we often experience it. According to Henry David Thoreau, "the mass of men lead lives of quiet desperation." He adds, "What is called resignation is confirmed desperation." I agree.

A touch of desperation, though, can be healthy and normal. Actor Jim Carey shares that, "Desperation is a necessary ingredient to learning anything, or creating anything. Period." Carey adds, "If you ain't desperate at some point, you ain't interesting."

The antidote to desperation is inspiration. In our fight against desperation, we can be inspired. Harry Shearer, another actor and comedian, shares that, "Nothing brings on inspiration more readily than desperation."

The word inspire comes from the Latin word *inspirare*, which means, "to breathe." Breathing requires two things—breathing in and breathing out. You have got to do both. A leader is seen as some who is really good at inspiring other people—breathing out. We should all desire this, but in order to breathe out a leader must also breathe in.

At SimVentions, I've found that breathing in is critical to our personal well-being and for our team's culture and commitment to excellence. What you take in is also what you put out. And there are four actions leaders can make to be inspired. These behaviors are illustrated in Figure 17.

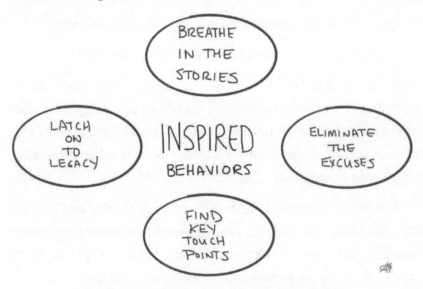

Figure 17 - Behaviors to Stay Inspired

Behavior 1 - Breathe in the Stories

There is an old song by the classic rock band Chicago that intrigued me. It's a song that frames a discussion between two individuals who have different perspectives and views on life and world events. Both are describing the same world, yet one shares concern, worry, and apprehension, whereas the other reflects contentment, excitement, and satisfaction. One sees the world as complex and confusing, whereas the other sees the world as more simple and clear.

The song is titled "Dialogue (Part I and II)" and there is a question in that song that the pessimist asks of the optimist that resonates with me—it inspires me to persevere. "Will you try to change things? Use the power that you have, the power of a million new ideas?"

I believe this question is an invitation for us all.

By the end of the dialog, there is a new perspective that melds both views. From the two different views—desperation and satisfaction—there comes a new view—inspiration. The second half of the song moves from dialog to anthem motivating the listener with three significant proclamations worth sharing: "We can make it better! We can change the world! We can make it happen!"

These proclamations reflect the belief of a leader who is ready and willing to persevere. One example of this is Elon Musk, the young entrepreneur who came up with the idea of PayPal. Today, Musk is revolutionizing the car industry with Tesla Motors and commercial space exploration with SpaceX. He has made an impact because he has been able to see something beyond the present, and he has been committed in his persistence to bring it to bear.

His achievements, so far, include commercial rockets that can orbit the earth and dock with the International Space Station, cars without dependencies on gasoline, and batteries that store energy long term for automobiles, homes, and businesses. All three of these achievements, which he continues to improve upon, were unlikely dreams and ideas to others. Many thought it was impossible. Yet, it has been through relentless perseverance that allows Musk and his team to create a revolution.

How did this happen? What made the difference for Musk that others have missed?

Believe it or not, Musk credits books to some degree for his success. As a young adult, books inspired him, and affected his outlook. They allowed him to dream. A common element of the heroes of the books he liked to read is that they "always felt a duty to save the world," he told *The New Yorker* in an interview in 2009.[59] One of those real life heroes for Musk was Benjamin Franklin. In his reflection of Walter Isaacson's biography of Franklin, a book that greatly inspired Musk, he shares his excitement.

"Franklin's pretty awesome," He reveals. "You can see how he was an entrepreneur... [Franklin is] one of the people that I most admired. He started from nothing, created his printing business, and then over time he also did science and politics."

Books on Tesla, the great scientist and engineer, also inspired Musk. That is perhaps is why he named one of his companies, Tesla Motors, after this great scientist.

Elon Musk is an example of someone who has made an impact by his commitment and dedication to a worthy cause or idea that once seemed impossible.

Magician David Blaine, who makes a living out of defying the odds and persevering shares that, "the only restrictions on our capacity to astonish ourselves and each other are imposed by our own minds." Breathing in stories allows us to be inspired. Breathing in stories allows us to explore beyond what's imposed by our own mind, and learn to persevere to make the impossible possible. We know this from the stories we read, whether biographies or works of fiction. Stories that inspire us, allow us to dream big, and relentlessly persevere. We learn that if they can do it, then we can do it!

Behavior 2 - Eliminate the Excuses

The perseverance found in the likes of Elon Musk or Benjamin Franklin should be a trait for the living and those who want to lead. Imagine the impact you could make if relentless perseverance was a trademark quality identified about you.

Unfortunately, very few people choose to maintain a perseverance mindset. While we marvel at the relentless perseverance found in others, we tend to not pursue it for ourselves and settle for comfort instead.

Why is that?

There are four toxic excuses that might keep us from persevering. Three that are ostensible reasons wrapped in the common phrases of the day, and a fourth rarely uttered but perhaps often considered. All of them are the result of limiting beliefs that can keep us from having the perseverance mindset.

- Excuse #1 – "No thanks. I'm good!"

- Excuse #2 – "No. There's got to be an easier way."

- Excuse #3 – "No Worries. There's always tomorrow."

- Excuse #4 – "No. I'm afraid I'll get what I ask for."

Benjamin Franklin once said that, "He that is good for making excuses is seldom good for anything else." There is no subtleness in his point, is there? That's because excuses minimize your effectiveness – especially as a leader.

Let's take a moment to explore each of these four toxic excuses.

Excuse #1 – "No Thanks. I'm Good!"

Have you ever heard the saying "if it ain't broke, don't fix it?" Sure you have. I know I've said it more times than I can count. But a house still needs preventive maintenance from time to time, right? If you wait until something's broken to fix it, it has the potential to become a bigger headache. The best hotels in the world, like the Orlando World Center Marriott where I'm currently writing this text, know that they have to stay on top of things before things break down. For a hotel to be the best, they have to relentlessly persevere to monitor and make the needed improvements before things get dilapidated and run down.

The US Navy aims for the same thing when it comes to maintaining its fleet of ships and aircrafts, so that they can stay the strongest Navy in the world. A ship out at sea has to be ready for anything, and for it to be ready for anything, all the equipment needs to be checked, and if possible replaced, before parts go bad.

Think of the airlines you choose to fly. They know if they don't stay on top of the aircraft maintenance, bad things can happen. Each plane needs to fly as if it did when it was first put into the fleet. You want parts replaced before they break.

The "No Thanks. I'm Good!" approach to life is often a reflection of an individual or a business simply content with where they are. There is little interest in taking time to maintain and re-equip elements to their personal life or business.

Excuse #2 - "No. There's got to be an easier way?"

No matter the struggle or the difficulty of the dream, we prefer success to come through minimal effort or through the fortune of a blessing or a miracle. We desire short over long, easy over hard, and minimal effort over an effort that requires perseverance. I'm no exception. While I've always been drawn to those who persevere, like others, I still wished for shortcuts to success. Yet far fewer achieve success through shortcuts than those that persevere.

For some, perseverance runs contrary to safety and risk. We think that relentless perseverance is going to take us out of a place of safety and put us somewhere we don't want to be. Perseverance can lead us to vulnerability, but the truth is you are more vulnerable if you don't move than if you do!

Excuse #3 - "No Worries. There's always tomorrow!"

Napoleon Hill once said, "Procrastination is the bad habit of putting off until the day after tomorrow what should have been done the day before yesterday." His comment makes me laugh! But it's true.

Legendary hockey player Wayne Gretzky stated it even more to the point when he remarked, "Procrastination is one of the most common and deadliest of diseases and its toll on success and happiness is heavy." Victor Kiam adds that, "Procrastination is opportunity's assassin."

If we know procrastination is deadly, then why do we do it? Why do we still procrastinate? This is a question I've wrestled with since I was in high school. That's because procrastination is something I've struggled with for a long time. It's been my Achilles heel.

If you are someone who procrastinates too, know that you're not alone. There are a lot of us out there. Even though we might procrastinate, I know that none of us like to do so. It's a trait we're not proud to have. Our intentions are never to procrastinate. Like everyone else, we'd much rather get the work done early. But, much to our chagrin, it often does not happen.

So, again, I ask the question, why do we procrastinate? What's our real excuse?

It's taken a while to find out, but I've found that two things can happen.

1) We let other things get in the way. Things that are just more interesting to us, albeit not as important.

2) We let fear and dread get in the way. We dread the effort. We fear not getting it perfect.

I want to focus on this second item a bit more. Perfection is just an excuse for procrastination. It's one that I'm often guilty of in my behavior. I want to get it right. However, when we fear not getting it perfect, then essentially our fear is getting out of the box, of getting exposed, or having our candle lit. To many, a lit candle can be messy. Wax drips everywhere. The flame might go out far from the box. The worry is that what might be worse than being in the box is being alone outside of it. Maybe we even fear success!

For me, procrastination is a combination of dreading the work—where I save the toughest stuff for later—and then trying to make it perfect. When it comes to procrastination the best way to overcome it is to identify what you really fear and face it. Admit to yourself and others what fears are keeping you from moving forward, and not use your habit to procrastinate as an excuse. Then, once you name the fear, face the fear head on. In other words – MOVE! Even if it's one small step. If you stand too long thinking and don't take that step, that might land you in the middle of the next common excuse.

Excuse #4 – "No. I'm afraid I'll get what I ask for."

Basically, what we are saying when we have this thought or make this excuse could be reworded as follows, "If I ask for the strength to persevere, then I'm going to be really tested and life could change and change for the worse."

Well, there's some partial truth to this belief. Perseverance will shift you from a state of idleness to a state of activity. It will change your circumstances and life will change. Our fear is that life will change for the worse, but you have to ask yourself, "Are you really so content with where you are now? Do you really want to stay in the box—not fully living to your potential?"

When things seem to be going well, the last thing on our mind is perseverance. It's simply not a request we're anxious to pray about. For if we do, we silently fear finding ourselves forced to persevere through a struggle. Even if you and I don't seek that strength or pray that prayer, challenges will still come, won't they?

Why not pursue perseverance independent of the circumstance in both good and bad times? Why not make perseverance a habit to living?

Instead, what if you turned those four excuses completely on their heads and allowed them to be bullets of inspiration. Instead of the excuse, let your response be an affirmation to persevere. Table 3 contrasts the two perspectives. Take a moment to evaluate the impact of an affirmation.

Table 3 - Perseverance Excuses and Affirmations

Perseverance Excuses	Perseverance Affirmations
No thanks, I'm good.	Yes, I am good, I am pressing on.
No. There's got to be an easier way.	Yes. There's no better way forward than pressing on.
No worries. There's always tomorrow!	No worries. I'm on it today!
I'm afraid if I ask for the strength to persevere, then I'm going to be really tested (and life will change and change for the worse.)	I'll always seek to persevere, life will change and that's ultimately for my benefit and others.

Perseverance is what separates the doers from the dreamers. It's what leads an individual and teams through the struggle to success. No one ever found success by having an excuse. Get inspired instead by holding onto these perseverance affirmations.

Behavior 3 - Find Key Touch Points

One morning as I sat down to write in my journal, I began to think about my limiting beliefs and my excuses that kept me from persevering. I contemplated other ways we can rid ourselves of our limiting beliefs and eliminate the excuses. Beyond the four perseverance affirmations, I wondered if there was something else that can help light the candle and keep the flame burning.

As I began to think about it, two questions formed that provided the answers for which I was looking.

- What inspires me?

- Who inspires me?

When I began to contemplate these questions, I realized I had stumbled onto something. I realized these are the questions that leaders ask to stay fresh and stay focused.

Being inspired awakens feeling, keeps us fresh, and helps us focus. Being inspired takes us from a state of complacence to a heightened state of awareness and courage. One of the things that can inspire us is a *touchpoint*. Touchpoints are tangible or visual elements. They can be a picture, quote, award, book, song, or photograph of a historic figure, a mentor, or a coach.

Touchpoints can help breathe life into you. They reflect people, places, and things! They encourage you to give a greater effort, to serve with enthusiasm, and to be creative. We need touch points to gently remind us of our mission and our message. Touchpoints can draw out the reason we should persevere, and the values we hold dear.

And the discovery of touch points centers on these two questions: What inspires you and who inspires you?

What Inspires You?

I love this question. If you want an icebreaker for your next team meeting, ask them that. You might be surprised at the answers you receive. Maybe your own answers will surprise you too?

As for me, I begin to think about tangible things that give me a shot in the arm. Music. Pictures. Memorabilia. Stories. Books. Movies. Quotes. Humor. History. Patriotism. Vacations. Great cities. Nature. Kayaking. Hiking. Skiing. Snorkeling. I could go on. Each of these in some small way can have a huge impact on me.

Let me pull on music for a moment. Sometimes all I need is the right song at the right time that will give me the energy to persevere. It might be the soundtrack to an epic movie such as *Gladiator*. It might also be electronic music, perhaps something from Zedd or Hardwell. Another favorite source is contemporary Christian music featuring a wide variety of styles. It might start with TobyMac, Tenth Avenue North, or Newsboys. Or it could be well-crafted contemporary worship music such as what you might find from Chris Tomlin, Matt Redmond, or Lifepoint Worship. Last but not least there's classic rock and roll featuring the likes of Boston, the Eagles, Kansas, Elton John, The Police, U2, or the legends of Motown. Sometimes nothing can give you more of an emotional boost that a popular song from the past.

How about you? Is there a song or genre of music that inspires and gets you moving and motivated? Do you have a playlist that can be your soundtrack to life! Every great movie with perseverance as its plot often had a great soundtrack. Maybe you deserve one too! After all your life is a story of perseverance!

In addition to music, there are other things that inspire me to persevere too. Some of the movies that grab my attention include *Remember the Titans, The Martian,* and *Gladiator* to name a few.

I also have some fantastic books on my shelf that keep me inspired. I'm particularly fond of the books in the Bible written by the Apostle Paul; *Philippians* is one of my favorites. I also have my shelves stocked with books that I often revisit. They included books by Seth Godin, John Maxwell, Daniel Pink, Dr. Henry Cloud, and Simon Sinek.

I encourage you to take a personal inventory of what inspires you. Keep these things in mind and keep them within reach so that you can stay inspired. They are touchpoints. Touchpoints allow you to *breathe in* so that you can more easily *breathe out!*

Who Inspires You?

From the dawn of time, the stories of success and great works have centered on a common theme of perseverance. Consider the perseverance required by explorers like Christopher Columbus or Sir Edmund Hillary. Their pursuits were epic. One found a new world; the other found the top of the world. Their stories and many others inspire us to persevere. I heard it once said that, "Great works are performed not by strength, but perseverance."[60]

When the question is asked, *who inspires you?* It might be explorers like these that come to mind.

Consider also the perseverance reflected in biblical characters like of David, Ruth or the Apostle Paul.

David was a shepherd boy, who became a king, but not until after he slayed a giant, and was almost eliminated by the prior king—whom he served and who was his best friend's dad.

Ruth, a young widow, endures hardship having to move across the country and work in the fields of a relative just to get by. She perseveres and is always a faithful and loyal servant. Eventually she catches the eye of Boaz. Her perseverance and faithfulness pays off and she falls in love with and marries Boaz and later they would become great grandparents to King David.

The Apostle Paul, who wrote most of the letters found in the New Testament, was blinded, shipwrecked, persecuted, beaten, stoned, bitten by a poisonous snake, and jailed multiple times. But he kept pressing on. His perseverance resulted in lives changed affecting every generation since. He is long gone, but his mission, his vision, his purpose is still having an impact today. It is his statement, which is the epigraph for this book that has motivated me and many others. "But one thing I do: Forgetting what is behind and straining toward what is ahead, I press on toward the goal to win the prize..." He considered life as a race. Not a rat race, as we might think of today, but a race worth pursuing and finishing strong. And he knew the impact perseverance could have on others who were followers of the Faith.

Consider also the mesmerizing tale of perseverance written about in Homer's *Odyssey*, where Odysseus endures a ten-year struggle to return home to his wife and son. Revealed to us in this epic story are Odysseus's *strength*, *bravery*, and *cleverness*. Three traits that inspire us—making us think we can possess these traits too.

Each of these stories has a common denominator. They center on perseverance amidst a struggle. For me, it is a reminder of one thing; we are made to persevere even in the face of difficulty. It's in our DNA. And when we hear and see stories of those who struggle yet persevere, they inspire us to do the same.

The question to ask again is, *who inspires you?* Take some time to the think about this question. Start by writing the names that first come to mind. Go back as far as you need to. The names themselves are touchpoints.

Behavior 4 - Latch onto Legacy

There is a number of people who come to mind that inspire me. I could try to list them all, but there is one specific name that stands out above the rest—my dad, Captain Arthur R. Gustavson, USN (retired). I am sure if you had known my dad, I think he might have inspired you too.

One of my earliest recollections of being inspired was as a toddler living at Great Lakes Naval Base. One afternoon, my dad came home early. I was supposed to be taking a nap, but when I heard his voice after he entered the house, I wanted to let him know I was awake. So I made enough fuss that soon my dad came into the room to rescue me.

When he entered the room I remember being captivated by his uniform. He was wearing his white Navy officer's cap and his black service uniform with gold trim. He came over and scooped me up from the crib. My eyes were locked on the medals and ribbons adorned on his chest. It was impressive. I grabbed at them, and gestured to him that I wanted to clutch them.

I have no idea what he said, but I remember him smiling at me as he gently pulled my hands off his uniform. As he sat me down on the floor, he removed the white cap from his head and placed it on mine. It was a touchpoint. That moment was magical for me. Like any young toddler, I loved my dad because I knew he loved me. He was a giver!

Called Home

Fast forward forty years later, my brother and I found ourselves desperately trying to find our way to Colorado from the East Coast. My mom had called just hours earlier from a small rural hospital outside of where they lived with the news that my dad might not make it. All of his organs where shutting down and the prognosis didn't look good. It was a total surprise. I had just talked to my dad a few days earlier. He had been battling an illness that was taking its toll, but we thought he'd pull through. We didn't know it was life threatening until now.

Within two hours of the call, my brother and I found flights to get out there. When we arrived in Philadelphia to catch our second leg, my cell phone rang with the news no one wants to hear. My dad had passed away.

My brother and I sat zombie like at Philadelphia airport for the next hour and a half. We were confused, shocked, and scared. As you can imagine, we weren't expecting this at all. Our life had just exploded into a million pieces, and we had no idea how we were going to be able to put it back together.

It wasn't long before we caught our next flight to Denver to go see my mom and help make funeral arrangements for my dad. That was the toughest trip I had ever made.

Later, after my sister joined us, we headed off to see Mom, driving from Denver to the small town of Buena Vista. Our emotion in the car was all over the place for the next two-and-half hours. We shared our favorite memories of him. Each of them was a beautiful illustration of a man that loved us as much as he loved life itself. We cried. We laughed. We sat silent. And we prayed.

No one on the planet believed in us more than our dad. Every time there was a new challenge in front of one of us, a new twist in our story, or new accomplishment, he was always available to listen, to encourage, to pat us on the back. Our stories of Dad were the stuff of legends, but we hadn't recognized it until after he had passed.

It's from my father that I learned that, "Success has to do with the effort and perseverance you make while you are living so that a lasting impact can be left behind when you are not." However, it wasn't until a few days later at his memorial service that I fully understood this truth.

We didn't anticipate very many people would attend. After all, it was a Sunday afternoon only a few days after he had passed, and people had probably already made their weekend plans. We were all pleasantly surprised. The church where the memorial was being held was at near capacity. People had come from all over the state.

My sister, brother, and I got a chance to share a few words. We reminisced of our father, a former Navy captain, a soccer coach, Church deacon, and a loving dad! We shared about a man who persevered in every sense of the word, from fighting for his country, to fighting prostate cancer, and to always fighting for his family, his church, and his community through prayer and active service.

After we spoke, others came up to share. The stories that we heard left us speechless. They shared stories of how he encouraged them, gave to them, shared with them, served them, and broke bread with them. Story after story gave us an even bigger glimpse of this man—our dad—and how he poured his life into others, just as he poured into us. In some ways, there was no big surprise. We had seen the character of Dad for ourselves. He was a true giver. But little did we know that same character was seen by so many others in a town that he had only lived in the past six years of his life.

Arlington National Cemetery

A few months later he was buried with full military honors at Arlington National Cemetery outside of Washington, D.C. In a word, the ceremony was epic.

At the Fort Myer Memorial Chapel, before the graveside service, I was asked by my mom to speak on behalf of the family. The words were easy yet hard. As I stood at the podium, I looked down at his flag-draped casket that was positioned between me and the chapel pews where everyone sat. The deep red and blue of the flag was vibrant and beautiful. I realized I wasn't just about to speak about my dad, I would be speaking for my dad.

I shared about how he was a gladiator, a fighter, a person who would fight for you because he believed in you, because he loved you.

"If he could speak to you today, he would tell you "to keep at it, to keep going no matter how tough the journey, to stay the course. He would tell you that God loves you and has a plan for you, a hope and a future."

I closed by sharing that "the world has been forever changed by the way he led and loved, and I believe that the best way to honor my dad would be for us to do the same! Let us lead to love."

Afterwards my family and I walked behind the horse-driven caisson carrying his flag-draped casket through Arlington National Cemetery. It was a warm and sunny December day, and the grounds were beautiful. Everywhere you looked you would see neatly lined marble markers memorializing those who served our nation. I couldn't help but feel their untold story of service, dedication, commitment and honor.

I thought back on his life even further. The pursuits he made as an officer in the Navy, the journeys he took, and the investments he made in the lives of each person of so many came to my mind. In that moment, I felt his presence and it seemed like others walking with me could feel it too.

A few minutes later, we sat as a family in the chairs by the graveside. The flag came off the casket and was folded neatly by the pallbearers. Then a Navy captain, a supply officer like my dad, gracefully walked over to my mom and placed the flag in her hands. While my brother and I were unable to cry in Philadelphia, we were crying in that moment—as were others. The captain then leaned toward my mom and shared this thought,

> Mrs. Gustavson, while I didn't know your husband personally, I am deeply touched by his life. It is truly an honor to be a part of this service and to wear the uniform as your husband did before me. It is an honor to follow in his footsteps. He will be someone I will

never forget. May God have comfort on you and your family.

At that moment, it felt as though my father was awarded a medal in heaven—another pin for his uniform. Only this one was labeled *saint*. A saint, according to the Bible, is someone set apart for the Lord and His kingdom. They are honored for their service in building up others.[61] Saints are the type of people you never forget, because saints still inspire well after they are gone.

That flag, that moment, and his tombstone marker are all touchpoints for me and my family. And as I sit down to write this text, I can almost hear him whisper one more time.

"Success has to do with the effort and perseverance you make while you are living so a lasting impact can be left behind when you're not."

Quietly, one more thought comes to mind that seems to put it all in perspective that I can only attribute from my dad.

"Make your life count for those who follow you."

That thought alone is enough to keep me inspired! That is why I wrote this book.

Wrap Up

The question to ask is, "what inspires you?"

The follow up question is, "who inspires you?"

Are there stories that you breathe in that are touchpoints that can impact you? Imagine what would happen if you were able to hold onto those touchpoints and the people who inspire you.

Let the stories that you breathe in, the touchpoints you've identified, and the legacy you desire strengthen your mission. If every day you connect with your touchpoints—not just look at them—but be reminded, then you will be touched in some way. You might be inspired again and again. It's then that you should ask yourself, *how I can turn this inspiration into perspiration?*[62]

One more thing, imagine how one day you might be a touchpoint for someone else who needs to be inspired. Remember, "Success has to do with the effort and perseverance you make while you are living so a lasting impact can be left behind when you're not." And while you are living, be strong! Because you never know who you are inspiring. It's in this way, you make your life count so that others are inspired to press on too.

Phase Four -
Discover the Bigger Picture

*Man cannot discover new oceans unless he
has the courage to lose sight of the shore.*

Andre Gide

T he great thing about exploration is that it leads to discovery. At this point, you have been well on your way—you have been walking the path. The discovery phase often produces the greatest feeling of satisfaction for a journey—a journey that most likely hasn't been easy.

Galileo, the great scientist from the sixteenth century who perfected the telescope and proved that the Earth and other planets in our galaxy circled the sun, famously remarked, "All truths are easy to understand once they are discovered; the point is to discover them." What you will discover when you persevere is the bigger picture; a destination perhaps far different and better than what you originally expected.

Even in this journey of reading this book, you are in a vastly different position and place than where you started. Because of that, you are likely going to need one of Galileo's telescopes just to see how far you've come.

Doesn't life offer more than what is expected? Confidence comes not by success but by the small steps you take along the way. It comes by your pursuit through challenges in finding a way to get back up. When you persevere the difference won't just be success but the significance that's been made in the lives of others. That is the mark of leadership.

This section highlights four of the elements of the bigger picture to be discovered for leaders press on.

Chapter 13 -
Expect the Unexpected

Nearly all the best things that came to me in life
have been unexpected, unplanned by me.

Carl Sandburg

E very one of us should expect surprises along the way. It's part of the journey. And every surprise, as grim as it may feel, could ultimately be a payoff—a payoff that energizes you, unites your team, and inspires others. The key is to embrace surprises as potential opportunities. Opportunities that are worth exploring.

The question though is how? How do you embrace surprises as potential opportunities? It's certainly not easy. When surprises come they can cast a dark shadow on your world; they are disruptive and they can be a blow. At a minimum, surprises seem to curb creativity, kill momentum, and cloud your vision. However, recognize you can't see the complete picture and understand the full path of your mission until after the journey. Hindsight, as they say, is 20/20 and surprises as you look back were often those little things that made all the difference. Therefore, rather than letting a surprise be a boulder that blocks your way, let it be a stone you can step off of to carry you further on your mission and refine your vision.

Looking back, I can see how embracing new challenges has played a critical role in building and shaping me and others. These challenges include not just the birth of SimVentions but other times too: completing college, forging relationships, pursuing new work, pounding through projects, dealing with health challenges, working through parenting challenges, and more. Our stories offer a burden of proof; a powerful testimony that perseverance is the greatest tool in the leadership toolbox.

My first big challenge that stands out specifically is what happened to me when I was in high school. It's from this story that I first learned of the payoffs that result from the *unexpected*, and how we should go about pursuing them.

Every leader can prepare for the unexpected by recognizing the four states of a great discovery. These states are illustrated in Figure 18.

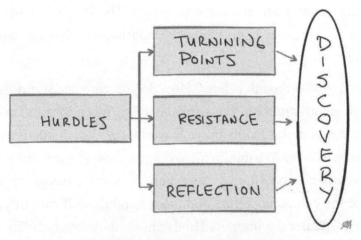

Figure 18 - Perseverance States

State 1 - Anticipate the Hurdles

In my junior year of high school, the unthinkable happened. On a brisk March Monday, a day that was slightly overcast and windy, I was on my way walking to varsity soccer practice. Just before I got to the field, my coach intercepted me to deliver a blow I'll never forget.

He led me away from the sidelines to get enough distance from my teammates. I was curious and wondered if he had something positive or something negative. I had no idea. But he had my attention. I was anxious to find out.

He took in a deep breath and shared what was on his mind. "Paul. I'm glad I caught you before you put your cleats on," he paused taking in his next thoughts. "I didn't realize you were going to make it out to practice today. I thought you might rest your leg today."

He was referring to an injury I sustained the Friday before. I had strained my hamstring during a drill that required us, for reasons unknown, to carry a teammate on our back doing a full sprint across the field. He assumed I was out for another day, but I was ready to be with my team. I had too much passion for the game to keep me away.

I smiled at coach and responded, "Yeah. I'm feeling better, Coach. I think I can give it a go!"

He then proceeded, "Well, glad you're feeling better. But I need to tell you something. And this may hurt a little." He paused for a brief second. "I need to tell you that I really don't have a spot for you on the team this season. I have two other guys in mind that are ahead of you on the depth chart for varsity, and I know the last two years on JV you played almost every minute of every game."

He paused. "This year, however, if I were to keep you on this team, you'd likely won't see much playing time." He then swallowed hard as I was trying to understand what he was telling me. "Paul, I'm sorry, but I'm going to have to let you go."

I was bewildered. "You mean I'm cut from the team?" I asked. My emotion started to show. I couldn't believe it.

"I afraid so," he said sheepishly. "The other two guys in your position are simply just faster than you, and I need speed at center defense." He then added, "And all the other positions are already accounted for. I've got who I need."

"What?" I responded. I wasn't ready to accept the news. "But Coach, there's only one other person that plays my position. That doesn't make sense. And I practiced with varsity all of last year even though I played in the JV games."

He had a ready answer. "Well, Sean is a freshman. He plays your position and I have slotted him ahead of you," He responded.

"Coach, you never call up freshmen. What do you mean?" I argued. I was showing a sign of emotion he hadn't seen before.

"Paul, my decision stands. I'm sorry!" Coach responded.

"I'm sorry too!" I muttered in defeat. I was angry, confused, and heartbroken.

His eyes lacked any empathy as he stared at me. It was clear he had made up his mind.

"Listen, Paul. I need to go. Thanks for trying to make it out today. I hope your leg continues to feel better," He said. Then he turned and left.

I stood there dumbfounded for a few seconds, but it seemed like eternity. I couldn't believe what had just happened. I then walked back home devastated. I had trained my whole life to play the game I loved and had aspirations to play at the collegiate level. Now all my goals were dashed. They were gone.

Embrace Fresh Starts

It took me a week to recover and pull myself out of victim-like thinking. My parents tried everything. My wall of soccer posters and pennants revealed my passion for the game. My life, my focus had been on the game of soccer since I young boy living in Brazil. The game was part of my DNA, and now it had been removed. And I didn't understand it.

My former teammates and friends were bewildered too, but they urged me to try something else. The only options were baseball or track. I wasn't interested in either.

But the victim mentality and pity party started to wear on my parents and through some of my teammate's encouragement, I chose track. I wanted to prove to my soccer coach that I could run with the best of them! That he was wrong about me!

A week after being cut from soccer, I was facing my new coach, Coach Windsor, the track coach. Since I was a soccer player, I thought I might be good at long distance. But after a few days of training with the team, Coach Windsor had other plans. He decided to make me a hurdler.

"Hurdler?" I thought. "I am not sure I can do that!" I told him.

"Oh, yes you can Gustavson," he bellowed, loud enough for everyone to hear even though he was only five feet away from me. Unlike my high school soccer coach, Coach Windsor wanted an audience when he spoke. "You might not have been a hurdler before I got you, but you are going to be one now!"

I could feel the eyes of the whole team on me sizing me up, wondering perhaps like me how I was going to be a contributor to the team at hurdles. I was the guy that got cut from soccer because I was thought not to be fast enough.

Obviously at first, I didn't share the same belief as Coach Windsor. I thought it was going to be a short-lived experiment. But Coach shot me a look that showed his resolve, which reinforced his earlier statement, "You're going to be a hurdler." He then handed me off to one my teammates to groom me. Marc Lerro was also a junior and one of the team captains. Helping Marc out was Bill Powell, who was a recent grad visiting the track that week while he was on his college spring break. Both had been seasoned all-district hurdlers and competed in regionals and states. I had yet to clear a hurdle in a race; they had cleared hundreds and had the medals to prove it. I felt intimidated.

"The first thing you need to do is work on getting your trailing leg over the hurdle," said Marc. He and Bill then lined up ten hurdles about a yard a part and showed me a drill focused on quickly getting the trail leg over each hurdle. First, Mark and Bill went and I watched. Then I tried and they watched. It was a rough start, but I eventually began to get it.

After ten minutes of that, it was time to run over a hurdle at speed. They marked off one hurdle about 15 yards from the starting line. Then they pulled out the starting blocks.

"Now we are going to work on clearing the first hurdle," Marc explained, as he and Bill set up the first hurdle and the starting blocks. Then Bill added, "It all starts with the first hurdle. You get to the first hurdle first then everything else is momentum."

Again, I watched them a few times come off the blocks and clear the first hurdle, and then run another 20 yards afterwards at full speed. Thirty-five yards total and just one hurdle. Then it was my turn.

After I set the blocks and positioned my feet in them, Bill clapped his hands to emulate a starting gun—the trigger to go! On his clap, I came out of the blocks and ran straight at the hurdle that Marc and Bill had placed in my lane. But that hurdle seemed like a brick wall to me, and so I bailed, going out of lane and running past the hurdle.

Then they had me go back to the blocks and try again. This time they dropped the hurdle even lower in height. Even though I told them everything was all right, inside I seriously doubted myself. In my mind's eye, all I could see was my left foot and leg going under the bar and me taking a horrible tumble. I tried to clear the thought out of my mind as I positioned myself in the blocks again. Once I was set, Bill clapped again. But this time I froze. I didn't go. I was afraid—wondering what I had gotten myself into.

Bill then came up to me and had me stand up out of the blocks. "Paul, the first thing you got to learn is to not to let anyone tell you 'you can't,'" he said, then added, "You can learn this just like Marc and I did. He and I were right where you are just a few years ago. You just got to trust the process. You'll get it if you just trust us."

Believe You Can

Coach Windsor had been watching the three of us from the pole vault area some forty yards away. After a while, he came up to the starting line. He interjected something I will never forget. "Gustavson. The only thing stopping you—is you!" His finger pointed into my chest. His message was clear. I had to believe I could!

Marc then came up to me as I positioned myself in the blocks for the umpteenth time. I was staring down at the track trying to get my sweaty fingers set on the starting line. He leaned down and simply whispered four powerful words to me. *"You. Can. Do. This!"*

Sure enough, it wasn't pretty, but this time I got over that first hurdle and removed a major obstacle that had been in my mind.

Looking back, I can see how that was the moment where Marc, Bill, and Coach Windsor were taking the flame from their candle and passing it on to me. They lit my wick. For me that sparked a sense of mission. I needed to prove to myself that I could, and prove to others, like my former High School soccer coach, that I could.

With a clear sense of mission, I worked to get my stride and steps down out of the gates and eliminate my stutter step before the first hurdle. Then, my job was just to work out my steps between the next nine hurdles. If I could get the strides right between hurdles one and two, I'd have it down for hurdles two through ten. Getting my steps right though was a lesson in frustration for the first few weeks of the season. But my teammates believed I could and, because they knew I could, soon I believed I could too.

What I've learned from that experience is this: How you start dictates how you ultimately finish. How you persevere dictates how far you can go. But your mission is what drives you. And the mission and vision can be transferable. It can be passed on by the sharing of a flame, which is what Coach Windsor, Marc and Bill did for me. Then once you catch your mission and see the vision, it can then also be the means for you to provide light to others around you.

Don't Lose Sight

While I was adjusting to a new sport, a new team, and a new challenge, the advantage I now had was a sense of mission. I was determined to do my best; to show that I had what it took despite the perceptions of my former soccer coach. Because of that, I was willing to learn.

In a month's time, I went from the clumsy new guy that ran his first race against Groveton in 21.6 seconds—which may have been the most embarrassing experience in my life and maybe for our team—to somebody who was contending for third place in the dual meets where we faced other schools in our district like Edison and Robert E. Lee. I was finding my legs, my stride and it felt great! I was earning points for our team and earning credit for my first varsity letter!

But then, just as I was getting comfortable and lessening my grip to grow, I began facing setbacks. The competition got stiffer. I put a lot of pressure on myself to do well. It was overwhelming. Soon I started clipping the top bar on the high hurdles, and my timing was thrown off. Instead of finishing third or fourth, giving our track team a point or two, I was finishing near the back of the pack. Zero points. That wasn't good enough for me or my team. My attitude started souring. I became less and less inspired.

Rather than continuing to ride the principles of perseverance that I learned those first few weeks, I reverted back to my old patterns. I let the challenges become setbacks, and doubt crept back in. Eventually the collection of setbacks became a major step back, and I wondered what my role was for the team. The words of my old soccer coach from just over a month earlier began to haunt me: "You're not fast enough!"

Quietly, I crawled back into my corner of safety with my head down, back into the box. I lost my momentum. Sadly, when you lose your momentum you can lose sight of your purpose. Without the patterns in play, "Knowing you can" becomes forgotten and you revert back to thinking you can't.

State 2 - Look for Turning Points

One track meet towards the end of that first season, I was having an off day. I was not running well; I was mad at myself and feeling dejected. We were going up against our archrivals, Mount Vernon, in a tri-meet that also featured Herndon High School. After what I thought where poor performances, I had isolated myself from my team. I had come in sixth in the high hurdles, and fourth place in the intermediate hurdles earning only one point for the team. Before the meet, Coach Windsor told me he was looking for me to finish at least fourth in the highs and third in the intermediates. But clearly I fell short.

Coach Windsor pulled me aside shortly after my two races were completed. About 20 minutes after the race he came to tell me to forget about what happened in the high hurdles that day and reflect instead on what I did in the intermediates hurdles—a race we called the 330 IMs.

"Paul, I want you to focus on the good you did in the 330 IMs. I like what I saw!" He said.

"But Coach, I only got fourth place. And I started off horribly," I countered.

"Paul, you were down in the 330 IMs. It wasn't your best start, but you made up for it in your finish," he added.

He went on, "You may have placed fourth, but you gave me more than a point. And you showed your teammates what heart and determination can do. That's what this team needs right now if we have any shot winning this meet!"

He held my interest as I replayed the race in my mind. I had started in lane six. Not a great lane to be in because you don't have the field of athletes in front of you due to the staggered starting lanes. In that race there were two lanes with runners in lanes seven and eight that were in front of me, and the runners in lanes one through five were behind me.

By the time I was a third of the way through the race, at the 110-yard mark, I had already let four other hurdlers pass me who were in lanes one through five. Things were not looking good. But then something happened; I dug in and found another gear. In the remaining 220 yards, I somehow caught up to two out of the four hurdlers who had passed me, and passed one of the hurdlers who was in lane eight. By race's end, I found myself finishing fourth, scoring a much needed point for the team. I was thankful for the excitement of my team, but I was bummed that I started so slowly and failed to get third place as intended. I felt I had failed.

Coach Windsor had a different perspective though, "Gustavson, you showed to me and your team just what can happen when you dig in and don't give up. That's what we needed from you today."

"Umm, thank you," I responded. I was blown away by his comment. It was something I needed to hear at that moment. It shifted my attitude!

Now, it's important to understand that Mt. Vernon had a great track team, and Coach Windsor had his eyes targeted on them all season long. He saw everyone on the team as a potential contributor to help us win against them. But, until that moment, I thought I had failed him. Then what he did next was beyond the expected.

He looked at me and give me some instructions. "Gustavson. Put your track spikes back on and warm up. You're not done today—and neither is this team."

"What do you mean Coach?" I responded.

"I need you to be ready to run the mile relay. You're running with Stackhouse, Lerro and Drummond—the junior team." Again, like the first day of practice, I questioned my coach. "You want me to run the quarter in the mile relay?"

"Yup! I do!" He replied. "We can still win this meet! And I need your heart on this one!"

"But Coach, other than practice, I have only run it once before. I'm not trained for it," I argued.

He then looked me dead in the eyes and said, "Son, I have been preparing you to run this since the day you stepped on my track five weeks ago. I want you to stop thinking about what you think you can't do and start doing what you can. I believe in you and so does this team. But you've got to believe in yourself first!"

I took what he was sharing with great interest. I had gone from discouraged and despondent to encouraged and excited in a matter of five minutes. My mindset shifted. I was ready to be bold!

"Lace up and get ready!" He said, walking away.

"What leg do you want me to run, Coach?" I hollered as he continued walking toward the track.

He turned his head and responded, "You're running second leg taking the baton from Stackhouse and bringing it to Lerro. Drummond is going to bring it home. Now go get with them! Time's a wasting."

The mile relay is one of the last races of the meet. As I was warming up with my team, I was dreading what I was about to do, but also excited about the opportunity and the belief that Coach Windsor had in me. Running 440 yards, the full distance all the way around the track, is one of the most difficult races at a track meet. It takes 100 percent of your effort for 100 percent of the race. It's basically a sprint from start to finish all way around the track. The muscles aren't equipped to run that long in a full sprint. At about two thirds of the way the oxygen in the legs and lungs seem fully depleted. For the last 110 yards of each leg, the only thing that seems to carry you is your faith and the cheering of the crowd from the grandstands.

Before every race I had run, I quietly said a prayer and recited Philippians 4:13, "I can do all things through Christ who strengthens me." Usually I'd pray this verse once my feet were locked in the blocks and I was positioning my hands on the starting line. But there would be no blocks for me this time. I had to be prepared to receive the baton standing up on the run.

As I stood off the track and watched my teammate Freeman Stackhouse settle into his blocks, I prayed my prayer—for him, for me, for the team. He held the baton firmly with his right hand, yet still having enough fingers to hold him up at the starting line.

I felt electrified. I was ready. We were ready!

At the sound of the gun, Stackhouse took off like a banshee. Our team started in lane four against five other teams who we were contending against. Our first team relay of four seniors in lane one, the two relay teams from Mount Vernon in lanes two and five, and two relay teams from Herndon in lanes three and six. At this point in the meet, we were down by just a few points. We needed a first and second place finish against the boys of Mount Vernon and Herndon. The odds were against us.

I thought if I had only gotten third in the high hurdles or the intermediate hurdles we would be in a better position to win the meet. But then I heard Windsor yelling at me as I was gearing up in anticipation for the hand off.

"Get ready, Gustavson. Just run it like you did the IMs!" Then his attention turned toward our first runner, Freeman Stackhouse. "Stackhouse, Go! Go! Go! Go!"

Windsor's voice was louder than a megaphone and it had brought my mind back to the race at hand. My teammate was in the lead running full speed. The two Mount Vernon teams where right on his heels, followed by the boys from Herndon. And our first team was right in the midst of them. All signs were showing that it was going to be a close race.

As Stackhouse rounded the final corner, I could see his eyes. He was laser focused on carrying the stick to me, and was putting out every effort in the world to get it to me. It would be a matter of seconds before he handed me the baton.

When he was about twenty yards away, I started to jog. As he got closer, I increased my speed, and my left hand went back ready to receive the baton. When it was neatly placed in my hand, I gripped it and bolted.

The words of Coach Windsor echoed across the track. "Go Gustavson! You got it! Go! Go! Go!"

The first 220 yards I felt great. No one had passed me. Then, as I rounded the second bend, two runners came on me from nowhere, and I felt myself fall into third place. One was a member from our first team relay team, and right alongside of him was Mount Vernon's first team runner. I felt like I was slipping away. But I was still churning.

Then I could hear the other runner for Mount Vernon's second team on my heels, and I was certain that not far from him was a runner from the Herndon team. I almost panicked and started thinking that I had lost the race. But then Windsor's voice bellowed again.

"Gustavson! You got this. Reel them in! Reel them in!"

I knew he was referring again to the 330 intermediate hurdles from the race earlier. He was now asking me to do what I had done earlier—reel them in!

When I came up to the grandstand in the quarter-mile relay, my legs felt like concrete and my lungs were about to explode. But the fans and my teammates in the stands where yelling like crazy. I had just 100 yards or so to go to hand off the baton to my teammate and good friend, Marc Lerro. I found my second wind, and soon the Mount Vernon runner that had passed me drew closer. As I entered into the handoff zone, I was nearly even with him, and then I handed the baton off to Marc.

Marc took off like a gazelle and made good ground. Soon we were in first place again, and our final runner, Ryan Drummond, had something to prove to our senior teammates. When he got the baton, he unveiled the speed that had drawn college coaches to come out to watch him and Marc that day. And in a total time of 3 minutes and 27 seconds, we finished the race in first place. Our senior relay team was slightly behind us, finishing second.

We had done it! We won the race and the meet. I could hardly believe it!

The four of us began high fiving each other and relishing about our win. It was an amazing experience. Coach Windsor came across to us with is big red beard and joyous smile. "Great job, men. You guys make me proud!" he said.

That was an amazing race and amazing lesson that I will never forget. It was a turning point. That race, that experience, and the wisdom of Coach Windsor taught me what I needed to discover.

- Be willing to learn and *grow*

- Be *ready* to run

- *Stay* inspired

- Be *passionate* all the way to the end

State 3 - Let Resistance Guide You

Shortly after that amazing relay, my teammates, who now had a new trust in me—and I in them—showed me that what had thrown me off before—clipping the hurdles—wasn't a sign of resistance; it was a sign of progress. They began to show me how the best hurdlers in the world just barely brush the top of the hurdle to help stay low and stay fast. I was also brushing the top of the hurdle, but I was letting it throw me off.

Sometimes we think resistance is simply an indicator that we are on the wrong path. But that's wrong. Resistance is there because you are on the right path. When you choose to persevere, you will discover that the resistance isn't there to stop you, but on the contrary, it's there to strengthen you and guide you and maybe even propel you on your way! I had no idea that skimming the hurdle was actually a good sign.

I had taken what I thought was adversity and an impediment and let it distract me. But my teammates shifted my perspective, they showed me how obstacles themselves can actually help you persevere.

It wasn't about jumping over the hurdle, it was about attacking the hurdle, and letting the lead leg glide over (maybe even touching the top bar) while the trail leg quickly rotates cleanly over the bar. It was about trusting that my strides and the steps where always going to be right and my goal was simply to stay focused on my lane, my cadence, and my drive to the end.

State 4 - Take Time to Reflect and Celebrate

To close out on this topic of understanding of how a surprise can be yield to a bigger payoff, I want to take you back to my Spring Sports Award Banquet, which culminated the end of the track season my junior year. It had been just four months earlier that my soccer coach had cut me by telling me I lacked the speed to play my position. That moment of rejection was painful. But there's an old adage that says, "When writing the story of your life, don't let anyone else hold the pen." Rather than letting my former soccer coach write my story, I had done something else to rewrite the story.

Originally, I chose to run track not because I needed something else to do, but because I needed to prove I had what it takes—at least to myself. The words of my former soccer coach all those months earlier had stung deeply, but tonight the sting had left.

Make no mistake about it though, track had not been easy. I stumbled at the start and there were times I thought I would never make it. Self-doubt was very active those first few weeks and throughout the season. But when you want to prove yourself, you persevere. The power of perseverance is what unlocks your story.

On that night of culmination, the spring sports teams gathered in attendance with their coaches and families to celebrate the season. Up until that point, I had made little contact with my former soccer coach, but on that night I wanted to causally bump into him. I wanted him to know the new story that had been written.

As the award ceremony got going, each coach shared something about their team and what they accomplished. Coach Windsor shared about his group of young men that fought to the end. He shared how proud he was of each of us and the effort that we gave to win the Gunston District and then make waves at regionals and state. But then he started talking about one of his athletes in particular.

"Tonight I have the honor to give out the award that is chosen for our most improved athlete. This is someone who stood out for all of us. Someone who fought day in and day out and always gave his best for himself and his teammates."

I sat there quietly wondering who coach was talking about.

He continued, "It was his first year of track. I didn't expect to have him on the team. He struggled at first, but by the end of the season he contributed greatly to our team, whether running a leg in the mile relay or giving us much needed points in the hurdles."

By then I realized he was talking about me, and I was numb.

"He improved not only himself, but his team. And it is my honor to recognize Paul Gustavson as this year's recipient of the Most Improved Athlete."

My breath was taken away. To this day, I don't even remember getting up out of seat. But I do remember accepting the award. I was in shock.

The smile on Windsor's face was genuine as I shook his hand He whispered to me. "Paul, congratulations. This is well earned." He then added, "I expect big things from you next season."

All I could say was "Thank you, Coach. Thanks for believing in me."

Needless to say, I was not the same young man as I was three months earlier. I had learned from my teammates what it takes to persevere. I had learned from my coach that my mindset starts with a simple step— "Hope in knowing you can!" I had learned that when you stay focused on knowing you can and combine that with perseverance, eventually you'll show yourself and show the world that you can!

And my "show the world that you can" moment—one of my proudest experiences as a young man—was that night. I had come to receive a varsity letter and a district patch for our team. But being recipient of the Most Improved Award meant that much more.

What I learned from that first season of track is that resistance doesn't choose for us whether we succeed or fail— this includes dealing with Grief and Pain. The choice is made by our decision to persevere in the midst of it. It comes back to our mission and having a vision. This is an important lesson I learned from Coach Windsor and my track teammates who collectively found a way to ignite my spirit.

I also learned something valuable from my former soccer coach. Even when someone doesn't believe in you, that doesn't mean you need to subscribe to their point of view. Instead, if you surround yourself with others who believe in the mission, and help cast the vision, you can overcome any hurdle. The key is to get out of the box, run the race, and keep at it!

John Paul DeJoria, the co-founder and face of Paul Mitchell, expresses it perfectly: "The biggest hurdle is rejection. Any business you start be ready for it. The difference between successful people and unsuccessful people is the successful people do all the things the unsuccessful people don't want to do. When ten doors are slammed in your face, go to door number eleven enthusiastically, with a smile on your face."

Dejoria is clearly stating that success comes by persevering and maintaining your mission despite rejection. And he underscores the importance of our mindset. Having the right mindset allows us to embrace those new challenges and transform what was once rejection into triumph.

Later that night, I bumped into my former soccer coach as I was walking through the foyer. We exchanged a few pleasantries, and then he took notice of my award that I was carrying.

"Congratulations," he said, and then looked over at my parents who were standing next to me. "You must be extremely proud of your son!"

Without missing a beat, my dad responded, "We are. He didn't let things keep him down."

Score one for my dad with that remark.

My former coach responded with a simple, but pleasant comment, "That, I can see." He then wished us well.

Perhaps that moment at first may have been an awkward exchange for my former soccer coach; I know it was for me. But in the end, it turned out to be impactful—it felt good. Any time you can receive an affirmation from someone who once doubted your ability, it can be a huge lift. I walked out of there knowing I had what it takes.

Wrap Up

Embracing new challenges is really a matter of being expectant of them. Expect the unexpected. When the unexpected happens, be open to the possibility that something better may come out of it. The infamous Marilyn Monroe once said, "Sometimes good things fall apart so better things can fall together." She's right. When good things fall apart, be ready and willing to adapt and try something different that might better fulfill your purpose. Sure your vision may have shifted, but your mission, which is how you lead, should still in play.

You seldom choose the challenges you face, but you do choose how you face each challenge. There are four states to remember to help you get through the unexpected: 1) Anticipate the hurdles. 2)

Look for the turning points. 3) Let the resistance help you. Resistance is there to let you know you're heading in the right direction. 4) Once you realize you are on the right path and making progress, take time to reflect and celebrate. This reinforces your behavior.

When you are willing to work through these four states you will find that you have been able to press on and have unlocked a new and better story.

Chapter 14 -
Harvest the Experience

We can only possess what we experience.
Truth, to be understood, must be lived.

Charlie Peacock
(attributed to A.W. Tozer)

O ne of the more impactful mindset principles in helping you persevere is having a thirst for experience. Experience is what turns knowledge into understanding. This value of experience though is often not fully understood until later in the journey.

Every person can discover *experience* to be an empowering tool in their journey by choosing to exercise three key tactics. These tactics are illustrated in Figure 19.

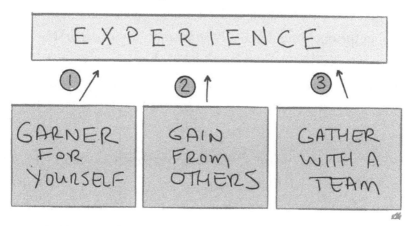

Figure 19 - Key Tactics to Harvesting Experience

Tactic 1 - Garner Experience for Yourself

The experience we garner can be a vital tactic in helping us persevere. Shortly after I graduated from college, I landed work as an engineer for a well-established software engineering firm supporting the US Navy. Early on there was little expectation from the management or my peers for me to step up and lead. As the new guy, my role was to sling code based on clear (and sometimes not so clear) requirements laid out for me, which was based on someone else's design work. For me, it was more like a data entry job—programmer, not engineer. No one was asking me to step into a role to be vision minded and to truly create. Eventually I realized I was settling in for boredom. While I was not being as creative as I wanted to be, I was simply happy to have a paycheck.

At that time, I was also into music. One artist that I enjoyed had several songs that were getting some airtime on the radio. His name was Charlie Peacock, and I decided to buy his new album called *The Secret of Time*. Over the course of a week, I listened over and over to the tunes as I drove to and from work. There were some great songs, but the one song that really stuck out for me and grabbed my attention was the last one on the album. It had a unique energy and passion that made me take notice the very first time I heard it. The lyrics intrigued me. I encourage you to read it not as a song, but as text.

"We can only possess what we experience. Truth, to be understood, must be lived. There is a difference, a qualitative difference between what [you] know as a fact, and what [you] know as truth. The facts of theology, though true in every way, alone can't change [you]. Truth, to be understood, must be lived. [You] can only possess what you experience."[63]

Those words made me think. Up until that point in my whole life, I just simply accepted the word of others as the truth. But facts and knowledge aren't truth until we try it and apply them.

I was thankful for the knowledge that I had gained and learned but I realized that unless I put that knowledge into practice, I wouldn't know its true value. Furthermore, I wouldn't know what I was capable of doing. What was the point of all those classes if I wasn't going to use them? I realized I had been trained as an engineer but was being used more like a data entry guy. I needed to be more proactive in what I was doing, and look to be more creative at work.

Additionally, the notion of only being able to possess what I experience intrigued me. It made me realize that what my paycheck allowed me to purchase and buy didn't have the staying power that experience would have if I sought it. My car, my music, my clothes, and my gear I had where temporal.

As they say, "Naked I was born and naked I will leave." However, the lyrics of that song made me realize there is one thing that I could hold onto that would last—experience. And experience was something that I soon hungered for. I wanted to prove myself as an engineer at work and see how I could lead.

I am sure you have heard the phrase, "You don't know until you try," right? It's true. You really don't know until you try. The two most disabling barriers to leading are our fears and limiting beliefs. And often they can be one in the same. Our fears and limiting beliefs keep us from our best version of ourselves; they keep us from pursuing the possible.

Yet there is one thing I know. If we seek out experience, we will find that we are capable of far more than we think. If we seek out experience, then fears start to fade and our limiting beliefs turn in into unlimited potential.

What's even more amazing is that experience, once you garner it, becomes part of your legacy—it can be passed down and shared with others! Remember, your life is your message.

So for me at that age, that song was a touchpoint that became a tipping point. I realized the importance of being proactive in doing things in my life like volunteering to present a topic at work, or explore a new way to add a software feature. Eventually I went all-in and pitched to corporate leadership a concept to develop a brand new real-time Windows application that had never been done before. Part of me thought I was going to be shot down, but the other part of me realized that I wouldn't know unless I tried. A month later, I had internal funding from the company for an innovative research and development (IRaD) project to develop the concept— a concept that paid some dividends for the company later.

That song changed my life, and the experiences I have today wouldn't have happened if it did motivate me to be proactive and garner experience for myself.

I want to encourage you too. Life is meant for more than sitting idly by. Part of your mission is to make the most of your life and take in what you can to understand all that it can offer. Truth, to be understood, must be lived.

Years later, I found out that the song was based on the work of A.W. Tozer. It comes from a short article where he talks about understanding God's truth is best understood by living it out, not just nodding in agreement regarding something that we read, heard and comprehend as truth. For you and me to value truth, we have to live it. Living out truth is the only thing that gives a leader experience.

Think of some of the leaders who possess expertise—Coaches like Tony Dungy, Herman Boone, Herb Brooks, and Innovators like Benjamin Franklin, Henry Ford, Thomas Edison, Elon Musk and many more. A leader with expertise is what is called a referent authority. These types of leaders are those who often have the greatest influence.

There are three ways to become a referent authority: Serve, Create, or Pioneer.

1) When you **Serve** other people or offer your service to a worthy cause the value you bring is often greatly appreciated and valued. The benefit of serving is that it connects with others. Serving helps leaders empathize and relate, thereby helping you (the leader) to understand and influence as you build your experience. As far as example leaders who are referent authorities, we'll explore two in a moment in the character Maximus and in the real Coach Herman Boone, the football coach from T.C. Williams High School featured in the movie, *Remember the Titans*. Both offer a great example of leader who served, gained experienced, and became referent authorities. As I consider the various mentors in my life, including my pastor, coaches, and my parents, they become referent authorizes because they served in some way. The value a leader is not just in who they have served but by how they have served

2) When you **Create** you discover the art of the possible. For instance, when you create you can begin to understand the laws of science and technology in a deeper way than you could in a classroom. When you create you'll find that you are able to harness the power of imagination in a very real way. The likes of Thomas Edison, Michael Jordan, and Bill Gates are examples that come to mind who became referent authorities because they learned to create what they imagined.

3) When you are a **Pioneer** you discover new horizons and new cultures. You develop an understanding of what enriches the world and those who live in it. The stories you capture hold treasures of truth giving you understanding that will eventually be sought by others. Great explorers that we can identify include Christopher Columbus, Steve Jobs, or Elon Musk. They are in many ways risk takers who have bent the status quo to discover something new and interesting and now forever stand out as a referent authority.

I encourage you to be a referent authority in your life too. Start with the passions that you have, and the interests that capture your attention. Consider how can you serve others? How can you create something new? What can you do to pioneer beyond the boundaries (and limitations) that others have defined? Remember, for truth to be understood it must be lived. You can only possess what you experience. Let your desire to understand be echoed by a desire to seek out experience. Experience can be the fire that lights your candle and helps you relentlessly persevere.

Tactic 2 - Gain Experience from Others

The experience of others goes a long way too. The best teams are those that have people who have been there before. The desire for experience is why we should have mentors in our life. There is something powerful about leaning into others who have the experience we don't have. For each experience there provides a fresh perspective, and if growth, readiness, and clarity is important for us, then experience should be too. It's a resource I want to have in my bag. The experience of others can make a huge difference to help me persevere.

In the previous section, we identified three different ways to become a referent authority: serving, creating and pioneering. The leaders that truly stand out seem to have a touch of all three of these qualities. Leaders who have garnered experience for themselves are the ones whom aspiring leaders can benefit from most. There are two stories that come to mind that reflect the impact a leader has on others when have they have experience. Both stories were reflected in two great movies: *Gladiator* and *Remember the Titans*.

Maximus

In the opening scenes of the epic movie *Gladiator,* we are introduced to the commander and general of the Roman army, General Maximus Decimus Meridius. Maximus is a highly respected leader and a loyal servant to the emperor, Caesar Marcus Aurelius. He is a warrior with experience, who is loyal to his men, and his men are loyal to him. Throughout the movie we bear witness to his character.

In that opening battle scene, we also find him preparing his men to take on the opposition—the Germanic army. Tensions are high. Archers and artillery wait in the open field ready to draw their bow. Before the battle commences, Maximus rides out to meet his infantry forces who are in the nearby woods awaiting his command. He has prepared them to flank the enemy while the remaining legion engages the enemy with flaming arrows and cannon artillery.

All the men know is that a battle is coming. In front of them looms a challenge, resistance, arrows, and swords. Some are ready, but most are scared. If you could ask any one of the men what drives them, they would have likely said that they are there to fight for Emperor Caesar—their king—and for Rome. But the truth is they fight for their general, their leader. His experience is like none other.

Maximus senses their fear. Just before the battle, he casts a mission to his men; a battle cry of perseverance that resonates with their heart and gives them focus. He addresses his troops.

"Three weeks from now, I will be harvesting my crops."

Maximus pauses for a second as he looks into their eyes. By starting with the end in mind, he has them captivated. Maximus is describing what's on the other side of their victory. He sees a favorable outcome.

"Imagine where you will be, and it will be so."

His comment casts a vision; a clear goal for them to aspire. Family. Peace. Home. Some of the men had lost that. But the men now relief in this image and have the incentive to persevere.

Maximus then raises his voice a little bit more, "Hold the line! Stay with me!"

All eyes are drawn to Maximus who sits on a horse ready for battle. He is telling them what they need to do in that moment to persevere. He is telling them that he will be with them in the battle.

"If you find yourself alone, riding in green fields with the sun on your face, do not be troubled! For you are in Elysium…and you're already dead!"

All the men laugh. They didn't expect that. The laughter causes a shot of endorphin, a powerful neurotransmitter that enters their bloodstream. The endorphin helps calm their nerves. Like other great leaders with experience, Maximus knows not only what needed to be said, but also when it needed to be said.

He is calm. He is confident.

Then, just before they prepare to advance, Maximus adds one more thought.

"Brothers!"

The laughter quickly fades. The chatter stops. He immediately has their attention once again. He continues making a statement of truth that echoes in my soul.

"What we do in life…echoes in eternity."[64]

The words penetrate deep. They resonate.

Then, in response the men shout with affirmation and excitement. They raise their swords in the air. Within them is a renewed hope and a purpose to persevere, a purpose that will stick with them into the battle—and well after. They are focused and ready.

Then the cue. Maximus's archers launch flaming arrows towards the threat. Upon this sign, the men advance forward on horseback. Their tactic is to flank the enemy. As they as they pick up speed, Maximus bellows. "Hold the line!"

The horses sense the adrenaline from the men. Without any necessary prodding they move faster. A few seconds later Maximus instructs them again. "Stay with me!"

The enemy is within a few hundred yards. As his men rush towards the battle, Maximus shouts out one last word of encouragement to his men, a proclamation of triumph just before the first clash of their swords.

"Roma Victor!" or "Rome is Victorious!"

This pre-declaration of the outcome might seem arrogant and brash, but for a leader like Maximus it is a way to inject hope and encourage perseverance. It is the way those with experience lead.

Like the soldier's in the movie, we are also drawn to leaders with experience like Maximus. He is a warrior leader. He is there for his men willing to impart his experience on others.

Later in the movie, he finds himself a slave who serves as a gladiator. Even as a slave we find that his leadership experience sticks out. It is because of his experience as a general that he and the other slaves are able to stand up against their enemy.

Maximus shows us the heart of a leader—they persevere. We want to be led by those who persevere, because it gives us greater confidence that we'll come out on top too. Leaders add value by sharing with us their experiences—experiences that come from both successes and failures. What we learn from them will help us persevere too.

The Real Coach Boone

Perseverance in others draws us in like a magnet. The experience of those who persevere is an appealing quality that makes us sit up, take notice, and follow. A great example of this is reflected in the movie *Remember the Titans* starring Denzel Washington, who plays Coach Herman Boone of T.C. Williams High School in Alexandria, Virginia.

In this story, based on actual events in 1971, we find a newly-minted football team struggling with racial integration from players brought in from two city schools. The players are at odds with each other. Coach Boone is faced with the challenge to unite the team. He also is facing conflict on his own coaching staff. Despite all odds, he pushes through the adversity and finds a way for the team to find a common bond. That common bond eventually transitions to success on the gridiron. The team begins to rack up win after win. They build momentum, and eventually they take the state title in 1971.

It is a mesmerizing story that keeps you on the edge of your seat all the way until the final credits. And it is an experience worth retelling.

My family and I had a chance to meet the real Coach Boone, along with many of the members of that championship team just a few years ago. The event started with an encore of the movie attended by Coach Boone, many of the actual players, and few of the actors from the movie. After the showing, there was a meet and

237

greet event at a nearby restaurant. I had a chance to talk with many of the players, including Coach Boone.

In my few moments with him, I shared with Coach that I had attended a crosstown rival school just outside of the city, Fort Hunt High School, and that we played TC Williams almost every year. He looked up at me from the table where he was signing posters and focused his attention solely on me. "You went to Fort Hunt?" he asked excitedly. "Those boys always gave us trouble. I'll never forget their one running back. What was his name? Rocky...?"

I laughed and interrupted him with the answer, "Rocky Belk."

"Yes! Rocky Belk," he fired back. "I remember playing them at their place in a monsoon. Rained all day. And Rocky was running all over us in the first half."

His former players around him begin leaning in to hear their former coach as if they were ready to strap their helmet on one more time. The experience of a leader always draws in his followers.

He continued, "But we had to come up with a special play to stop him. Still remember it to this day." He then grabbed a napkin and sharpie and proceeded to draw out the play. "We called it the 'Special Defense to Stop Rocky Belk'". He finished out drawing the play on the napkin, and dug his finger into it. "That's how we stopped him. But he was a great back. Great back. Went on to play at Miami, right?"

I replied. "Yup, he sure did. He played at the U."

Then he smiled. "Yeah, those where the good old days. And your school always fought us hard."

We exchanged a few more pleasantries, laughed a bit more, and then bid each other farewell. He then handed me the napkin with the infamous play drawn on it, which I have on display in my office at home.

Before my wife and I met Coach Boone that night, I had an image of him looking like the actor that played him, Denzel Washington. Truth is he didn't look anything like Denzel, but it was clear that like the talented actor that played him, Coach Boone was an original—a man who persevered as a leader and truly influenced those around him.

My wife and I ended up talking with other players that night, and also met one of the actors from the movie. It was an incredible evening meeting the real players of that team.

A thought struck me later as I reflected on that night. When you meet someone who has truly learned to persevere and they share just a tidbit of how they did it, it impacts you—it leaves a memory. The shared experience of a leader can inspire you leaving a mark of experience you can leverage for yourself. When an experience is shared it can take root in those that listen and hear.

As for his players, when you are under the leadership of someone like that, someone who has helped you persevere and accomplish something great, you are changed forever. If that weren't the case, then all those players would not have been with Coach Boone on that night.

Tactic 3 - Gather Experience with Your Team

The experience of others goes a long way too. The best teams are teams that consist of individuals who are willing to work together and share with one another their experience. There is something powerful about leaning into others who have the experience you may not have. A team will have your back, and they will help you gain the experience you need because you're giving them new experience too. Among these types of teammates, there can be fresh perspective and a contagious passion that will take you further than you could alone. Couple this with the experience you can gain from a mentor or a coach, and you'll go even further.

Wrap Up

Experience only comes by engagement. And the best engagement is having fellowship and accountability with one another. Garner experience for yourself. Gain experience from others. Then gather experience with your team. As Aristotle once said, "the whole is always greater than the sum of the parts." The combined experience will take you and your team further than you can imagine. They will help you persevere.

Our success at SimVentions, for example, isn't because of just one person or one lucky contract, it's because of a united team willing to share together, care together, work together, and play together by leveraging and valuing the experience that we have. If we ever stop valuing the experience that we have and that we should always be in the midst of attaining, then we become less than our best.

Mediocrity is a word that scares me. Experience garnered, gained, and gathered, however, is what trumps mediocrity. Experience is something to discover again and again and again. Experience will undoubtedly help you and your team press on.

Chapter 15 -
See What You Believe

If you're dealing with doubt, worry, anxiety, or fear in any area of your life today, faith is the antidote. [65]

Joyce Meyer

A long life's journey, I've discovered one thing to be absolutely true: to get to the finish, it requires faith. With faith anything is possible. Author and thought leader Brad Lomenick shares that, "A habit of faith is essential to your journey as a leader." He adds, "That's the part you can't leave home without."[66]

In Chapter 4, we focused on the first half of Saint Augustine's quote, which reads, "Faith is to believe what you do not see." That chapter was centered on the importance of persevering with hope. The second half of his quote is, "The reward of this faith is to see what you believe."

When we see what we believe, with faith we are able to move through distance and time and over unlikely circumstances. Face it; you can't see what's around the corner. Life is full of unknowns— good and bad. If we worry what's around the corner, we might not get anywhere. That's where faith steps in. At the end of the day, when we examine how we get to the finish line we should recognize that faith was absolutely necessary for our survival.

Faith is one of my favorite mindset principles because it's the one choice that can have the most impact in helping you persevere with the least amount of effort required. That said, it's also the hardest because it requires complete trust in something beyond your control.

There are four elements of faith that help leaders and their team's fight the good fight to successfully get across the finish line. Each of these elements is illustrated in Figure 20, and includes the six levels of faith that we will describe in this chapter.

Figure 20 - Faith Elements and Levels

Element 1 – Understand the Levels of Faith

There are six levels of faith that are significant in helping individuals, leaders, and teams persevere.

Level 1 Faith (Infrastructure) - There is faith in the infrastructure around us and technology and products we build. These are important to us, but unfortunately they are not always dependable.

Level 2 Faith (Physics) - There is also faith in science and in math. It creates clarity and helps us understand how the universe operates. Our knowledge of gravity, time, distance, and other laws of physics have helped us put man on the moon and satellites in space. But faith at this level can only get us so far. The secrets of the universe are far from all known. Rarely does science account for and anticipate the challenges that we face.

Level 3 Faith (Process) - There is faith in the processes and procedures we establish. This includes our government and judicial system. They are important to help give our lives structure and a sense of fairness, but they do not always seem fair, do they? They can disappoint us at times. In socialistic environments, they become far from fruitful.

Level 4 Faith (Leadership) - There is faith in the principles and laws of leadership and living. There is incredible wisdom in these principles and they will surely make an impact, however, they don't always guarantee success. The laws of leadership are based on the observations of man to date. There is still much to learn on how to lead and lead effectively.

Level 5 Faith (Relationship) - There is faith and trust in the people around you—including yourself. This is critical. It is important for followers to feel trusted by their leader and for them to trust you. However, because we are all human and we have different personalities and emotions, it can be difficult to get along with everyone. When there are struggles with one another, it makes it hard to persevere. But it is far easier to preserve with someone alongside of you than if you were by yourself. Faith at this level is very important. But we have to work at both giving trust to others and earning trust. Individuals and companies that are consistent in the production and service and who continue to persevere are those who earn our trust.

Level 6 Faith (God) - Finally, there is faith and trust in a deity that's greater than you or me. An almighty creator who knitted us, sustains us and loves us. For me, it's faith in a triune God: the Father, who created everything; the Son, Jesus Christ, who is the redeemer for everyone; and the Holy Spirit, who is the helper for anyone who is willing to trust in Him and persevere in this life.

This is the level of faith that can be the most trusted, but it's also the hardest. This level of faith is exercised in five steps. Prayer, Petition, Trust, Action, and Praise

Step 1) **Prayer** creates connection; acknowledging God's presence.

Step 2) **Petition** communicates the need. It identifies what you and your team are dealing with.

Step 3) **Trust** surrenders your worry to God with the belief the you (and your team) will be enabled to somehow get through whatever it is you are dealing with and remind you that you are not alone.

Step 4) **Action** is the outward behavior to trust. It is you (and your team) making movement to push forward through your challenge and effort despite the adversity, believing that that what you can control is be addressed and handled by God. Your part is to do what you can control.

Step 5) **Praise** is acknowledging God's involvement and His provisions along the way—not just at the finish line. It's thanking Him for his blessings in your life and your team's life.

These are the six levels of faith. I realize that all of us know someone that will dismiss the sixth level of faith as a necessary means to perseverance. If that's you, that is certainly your choice, however, the intent of this book has been to offer a framework to perseverance that centers on primarily the last three levels of faith: Leadership, People, and God. The framework has value independent of one's personal faith. However, do consider the impact that Level 6 Faith does have for others. I honestly couldn't write this book without sharing the importance of Level 6 Faith.

Element 2 – Create a Habit of Trust

Faith is about trust.

- Faith is trust in the assets around us. The chair. The steps. The car. The floor. The bridge. (This is Level 1 and Level 2 Faith)

- Faith is trust in the process and leadership laws. That the instructions, the methods, or the recipe will work time and time again. (This is Level 3 and Level 4 Faith)

- Faith is trust in ourselves individually. That we have the aptitude and the ability to accomplish a task or learn a new skill. (This is Level 5 Faith)

- Faith is trust in those around us. Our team. Our partners. Our customers. Our family. Our friends. (This is also Level 5 Faith)

- Finally, faith, for many, is trust and belief in God, the creator of this world we live on. (This is Level 6 Faith)

As a person of faith, I believe of all the things to trust, God is the most trustworthy—Level 6 Faith. I believe wholeheartedly that we don't walk this world alone. I have seen first-hand the effect of Level 6 Faith in almost every season of my life. For me, it's critical to my perseverance. It's the fuel that I need to keep my candle lit, and to offer light to others.

Faith can be instrumental for alcoholics and others with addiction to change their bad habit and "make it through the stressful periods".[67] Proof can be found in the stories and successes of hundreds of thousands of individuals have had through Alcoholic Anonymous program. Based on his research on habits, Charles Duhigg shares that it is the *belief* in God that makes a difference for an alcoholic. This belief is the center point of faith

It starts with a belief that change can take place. It's the belief in God that can be a key ingredient that changes habits and forms new, permanent, healthy behaviors. And its belief in God that spills over to other parts of our lives and makes a difference!

Element 3 - Measure Faith by Commitment

Perseverance is measured by faith. It's the cumulative value of commitment traveled from the starting line to the finish line. This cumulative value represents the amount of trust you had for any of the six levels of faith.

The question though is how can you persevere with complete trust across all the levels of faith? For example, who in your life would be perfect enough to warrant complete Level 5 Faith, which is trust in people? Humans are imperfect. We make mistakes.

Of all the levels of faith, the only one that I believe can truly be tested is Level 6 Faith. But recognize it's going to take some Level 5 Faith to go along with it. That's because God likes partnerships. He likes to send other people your way to help you persevere— that's how He prefers to work.

For me, I credit God as the author and finisher of my faith, and I also credit a great team that has helped me persevere along the way (Level 5), and great leadership principles (Level 4). I can count at least a dozen times where things that were going badly should have ended badly, but through prayer, patience or just divine intervention, they didn't (Level 6). And, often, others where there for support, for encouragement, and for casting a vision (Level 5). And the leadership principles have offered the mindset and mechanics needed to influence myself and others (Level 4). Faith at these three levels, has impacted me personally and professionally. SimVentions wouldn't have seen life if it wasn't for these levels of faith. It's a combo pack!

Consider your life up to this point as well. What has brought you this far? Has it been completely your effort, or have you gotten support from others including God? Isn't there just a little bit of a mystery to how you have come this far?

If the latter is true, could it be that the progression and sustainment of your life might be because of Level 6 Faith?

I am alive today because of the Level 6 Faith that others have exercised in my behalf through prayer and petition, which also credits Level 5 Faith. But let me just focus on Level 6 Faith for a moment. There have been some near fatal missteps on my part. The stories you read of a toddler drowning, a child falling, or a teenager succumbing to a mountain climbing accident are stories that could have and should been about me. I've come close more than once to seeing the end of life, whether biking, hiking, skiing, swimming, or driving. But I know the protection and perseverance that I have experienced can only come from God. Personally, Level 6 Faith is what has kept me going.

Professionally, I know that our business at SimVentions has been able to weather through multiple challenges and struggles over our short life because of God as well. He helped establish our business for a reason. Our faith has demonstrated that with God all things are possible.

I believe your story is similar. He has you here for a reason. Perseverance is an attribute of God. It's part of His nature. He won't give up on you. And, since you and I are created in His image, then perseverance is an attribute He desires of us to reciprocate. It should be part of our nature too. But we have to work for it. "If you want the fruit you have to go out on the limb to get it"[68]. Faith without action is dead!

But don't let the inactions of your past effect your *today*. Yesterday is gone! What matters is right now. What decision will you make to take a step of faith? What level of faith are you willing to trust? Are you willing to trust and live with Level 6 Faith? Consider the alternative. Living by only what you can see can be demoralizing and even deadly. Level 6 Faith relinquishes your need to know completely how you will get to the finish. Your job— and my job— is to respond with obedience by persevering and trusting God, and also be a contributor to Level 5 Faith for others!

Element 4 - Know What Ignites Faith

Often what can ignite our faith is a question to expose our intent. Questions that dare us to be bold and statements that challenge us to share our belief are what can change history. For me, it was the question, "But you still have hope, don't you?" This, again, was asked of me at a challenging time when I needed to be reminded of my vision. Both the question and the answer changed my trajectory. It fired up my faith.

MLK

The words of past leaders often still inspire us to do something great in faith. Consider Martin Luther King Jr.'s remarks given at the steps of the Lincoln Memorial in 1963. He eloquently shared, "Even though we face the difficulties of today and tomorrow, I still have a dream. It is a dream deeply rooted in the American dream. I have a dream that one day this nation will rise up and live out the true meaning of its creed: *We hold these truths to be self-evident, that all men are created equal.*"

In this infamous speech, he ended up mentioning not one dream but six dreams—all focused on his vision of freedom.

As King nears the end of his "I Have a Dream" speech, he introduces the ultimate vision of his dream—a vision that can only be pursued by faith. "This [Dream] is our hope. This is the faith that I will go back to the South with. With this faith we will be able to hew out of the mountain of despair a stone of hope. With this faith we will be able to work together, to pray together, to struggle together, to go to jail together, to stand up for freedom together, knowing that we will be free one day."

Don't miss the subtle hint. There were over a quarter of a million people in front of the steps of the Lincoln Memorial on that hot summer day in 1963, and I am certain he knew the rest of the world would be hearing the speech later that night. While outwardly he is talking about a dream of freedom, inwardly he is reminding everyone also the need to persevere together through faith.

His *I Have a Dream* speech were words for all Americans. It made us question our own dreams and aspirations for fellow man and humanity. That speech changed our perspective, and it changed history. It became a pivot of perseverance in America's ongoing pursuit of freedom.

JFK

Two and a half years earlier another leader of that era, John F. Kennedy, gave an aspiring inaugural address that also still inspires us today. In that inaugural address, he transitions from talking about the mission for freedom, to the role you and I play in supporting it.

"Ask not what your country can do for you, but what you can do for your country."

This statement still has impact. It makes us ponder and wonder, "What can we do to make a difference?" JFK then expanded this statement to the rest of the world.

"My fellow citizens of the world: ask not what America will do for you, but what together we can do for the freedom of man."

Just before JFK made these two statements, he was weaving his mission, and casting the vision. He was talking about freedom, and how important it was for him, for us, and for the world. He was sharing the importance to persevere and maintain it.

Like any great leader, he involved others. Consider also his words earlier in the speech. "The energy, the faith, the devotion which we bring to this endeavor (the mission of freedom) will light our country and all who serve it—and the glow from that fire can truly light the world."

Did you catch his key words? Energy. Faith. Devotion. Endeavor. Fire. Light. Those are words that ignite our faith. For me, it's a reminder that perseverance with faith can be something that will help light the candles of others.

Wrap Up

Faith isn't just a wish; it's acting on a belief. And the more of us that do it—act on faith—the more impact it will create. Faith coupled with prayer gives the strength to persevere. And in this regard, it is more impactful than any other mindset principle combined.

You'll discover that the reward of faith comes through trust. That includes first and foremost trust in God (Level 6 Faith); second, trust in yourself and others (Level 5 Faith); and third, trust in the leadership laws (Level 4 Faith). All three of these top levels of faith need to be in play. A response to faith by taking action at these three levels will enable you and the teams you lead to press on!

Chapter 16 -
Let Generosity Multiply

There is no exercise better for the heart than
reaching down and lifting people up.

John Andrew Holmes

Originally I wanted to end the book on the reward of faith. I thought that was the right way to wrap it up, but then I realized I would have left out a crucial component to leadership and business that multiplies everything else—generosity.

Generosity is a multiplier for every one of the mindset choices to perseverance. Leaders that are generous tend to grow more, are more ready for what comes, are more inspired, and have a passion that is contagious. These are all marks of perseverance.

Additionally, leaders that are generous tend to elevate the attitude of others and impart more courage—that is they encourage. They tend to also have greater clarity of the vision, and greater desire to complete the mission. Also, those that are generous gather more experiences to share, and tend to model their faith to others. Simply put, generosity multiples perseverance.

There is one more interesting tidbit. Those that are generous tend to be genuinely happier too. Christian Smith and Hilary Davidson, authors of the book *The Paradox of Generosity*, surveyed 2,000 people over a five-year period to explore the effect of generosity. Their study revealed that those who volunteer more than

5 hours a month or donate more than 10% of their income are more content and significantly less depressed than those who don't have a habit of generosity— in other words they are happier. It goes to show you that Mark Twain was right when he said, "The best way to cheer yourself up is to try to cheer somebody else up."

In addition, their study revealed that those who are generous in lifting others up are healthier than those who don't. The data shows that being generous can be an essential ingredient for happiness, health and perseverance.[69]

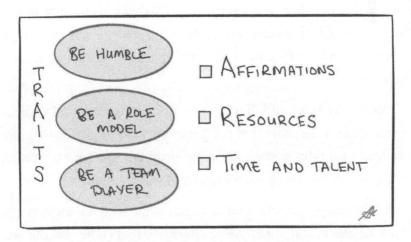

Figure 21 - Generosity Traits

The question, though, is what does it take to build generosity? The answer to the question centers on looking at the habits and patterns of leaders and philanthropists who have persevered and are generous. I've gone back and looked at the lives of Abraham Lincoln, Henry Ford, George Eastman, Warren Buffet, and Mother Teresa to name a few. All are known as leaders who have persevered, and are also known for their generosity. My findings reveal several behaviors and traits reflective of a generous leader. These acts of generosity are illustrated in Figure 21.

Trait #1 – Be Humble

According to psychologist Jordan LaBouff, "Compassion is hard if you don't have humility."[70] However, humility does not come easy for most leaders. For some, the perception is that humility forces you to think less of yourself. That it limits your skills and ability, and that it cripples your confidence. The misperception is that a humble leader is a weak leader. But C. S. Lewis defines it differently. He shares that "Humility is not thinking less of yourself, it's thinking of yourself less." Humility, the right humility, is a game changer. Humility allows you to touch lives and change lives.

Humility is a trait that needs to be learned and refined. One of the best examples of a leader who lead with humility is Abraham Lincoln. From humble beginnings he learned to listen and lead. He learned not to take anything for granted. *Psychology Today* reveals that, "Lincoln was a masterful leader because he was able to master his own ego first." It goes on to share that "Lincoln proved that any leader's first and greatest victory is always that over his own ego.[71]

Your ego can be what stops you, but here are a few tips to help you master your ego, help you stay humble, and ultimately help you lead well.

- Give credit to others
- Demonstrate patience
- Listen before you lead
- Display grace and mercy

These four simple actions can help set the frame for an effective and generous leader.

Trait #2 – Be a Role Model

Ultimately, at the end of the day, generosity should be measured by how a leader has helped others persevere, and that starts with modeling it. Humility sets the frame, but it's the actions that change the game. There are three essential practices to put generosity into play. I call it the ART of generosity.

- Be Generous with Affirmations

- Be Generous with Resources

- Ge Generous with Time and Talent

Notice that each of the keywords spells the word ART—Affirmations, Resources, Time and Talent. The concept is simple; we each have the knack and ability to affect change. It's an art form that can be learned for anyone who is in the role of a leader.

Be Generous with Affirmations

Coach Jack D. Bergen, my soccer coach before high school, was someone who looked to find something positive in each player that he coached. By day, he was a major in the US Army and later became a chief speechwriter to the Secretary of Defense, Caspar Weinberger. However, because he knew me as a player, he was the man I asked to share a few words on my behalf at my Eagle Scout Award ceremony.

I was fourteen years old when I received my Eagle Award, but I still remember the way he made me feel that night. Sharing affirming words of my character that he truly believed in. But what he did for me that night wasn't just a one-time thing. He spoke on "strength of character" for all the players he coached and for his two boys that he raised, John and Mike. He was a model for me—a true leader. And his generosity with words of affirmation wrapped in acknowledgement, approval, and encouragement still resonate with me.

At the end of one practice, I remember how he was speaking life into each of us. Our soccer team at that point was a blend of two groups; players that had been there since the inception of the team, and players that he recently added to the fold. He called one group *the survivors* and the other group *the saviors*. It was a turning point moment where he found a way for the new guys to feel like they had something to contribute to the team and feel welcomed. And it was also a special moment for players like me that had been around a while to feel like the best was yet to come. I can't explain the emotional high we each had at the end of that practice, but I can honestly tell you that as a team we had never felt more charged up and more connected.

The energy spilled over to the tournament play we had the next three days. Our team was a wild card at best to win the tournament, but Coach believed in us. And we believed in each other. It was the Columbus Day tournament, and I was excited about what we could do. We all felt that way. And each of us, individually, played at a very high level. There was little doubt in us. As a team, we worked hard to connect and distribute and encourage. That became one of our trademarks. We needed to encourage each other, just like our coach modeled for us with his words of affirmation.

In the championship game, we were playing well but so was the other team. The score was even at one a piece. Late in the second half, one of our players went down in their penalty box and we were awarded a penalty kick. I was playing defense, and Coach hollered out to me. "Paul, you take it!" I was confident yet nervous.

Earlier that summer, I had been at a camp at The College of William and Mary where there was a penalty kicking contest among 50 or 60 players shooting against college goal keepers. Several of my teammates and I competed in that contest. It was a big deal.

I survived each round scoring each time and then ultimately made the last shot. Winning that competition had been a huge morale booster for me, and Coach Bergen wanted to capitalize on that skill, so he designated me as the go to guy to take PKs. This was my first opportunity of the season – at least for a big game. Knowing my coach believed in me was enormous. In that Columbus Day championship game, I jogged up the field and one of my teammates, Mike, tapped me on my shoulder telling me, "You got this!" I affirmed myself with his words echoing the thought in my mind, "I got this!"

Before I took the kick, I looked over at the players behind me and then over at the sideline. There stood Coach Bergen giving me a nod of approval. He wanted me to net it. He knew I could do it! I also saw my dad just behind him off to the side watching the game, watching me. It was a great feeling to know he was supporting me too.

After the referee lined up the ball and made sure the goalie was ready, he gave me the signal to take the kick. I gave a slight glance to one side of the goal (hoping the goalie casually saw my look), but I visualized myself shooting to the opposite side—mirroring exactly what I just pictured. It was the same routine I had done at William and Mary.

Quickly, I came up and struck the ball firmly sending it exactly to the opposite side of the goal of where I had glanced. The ball traveled hard and fast. The goalie had anticipated my shot starting his dive toward where I had originally looked, but he had guessed wrong. As his hands and feet sprawled to cover the wrong side of the goal, the ball slipped by him on the opposite side striking the left side of the net. As the ball fell slowly back to earth, I watched the net wave like a flag in the wind as my teammates erupted with excitement.

As I trotted back to defense, I looked over to the sideline again and Coach Bergen had a big smile. His fist clinched in triumph. My dad was smiling too. It was a goose bumps moment, and I smiled back.

We held on to win that game, and it was a great feeling. We celebrated afterwards. But what Coach said to us all was what made a lasting impression. I took in his gaze as he summarized that championship moment for each of us.

> To the survivors and the saviors—today you were *one team*! Each of you gave it your all. Each of you proved to yourselves that you have what it takes! Today, I couldn't be prouder to be your coach! And I want you—all of you—to remember that any time you feel a struggle or face a challenge to never give up. Lean on each other. Let the moment of today and this trophy we won this weekend forever serve as

reminder of what teamwork and hard work can accomplish!

That tournament, that game, and those words have had a lasting impact for me. As I look back, our team's ability to persevere would not have likely happened if it wasn't for the affirmation Coach Bergen gave to us all along the way. I am thankful not only for his words of affirmation, but that he backed it up with trust!

Isn't it interesting that his affirmation back then still makes an impact for me today? Is the same true for you? Think of an encouragement or affirmation made to you by a leader in the past. Does it still make an impact for you today?

It's not a coincidence that many of the famous quotes and thoughts that inspire us today were given as an affirmation when they were first spoken or written. These quotes stand the test of time. It's a reminder to be generous. An affirmation or word of encouragement may help someone you'll never know.

Let your words of affirmations be an encouragement to others and to yourself. Let it be the default mode for generosity. Consider that it costs very little of your resources and very little of your time, yet it can have the most impact. Affirmations multiply perseverance for yourself and for others.

Be Generous with Resources

My wife and I enjoy kicking back from time to time to watch an episode of *Shark Tank* on TV. We find it a mesmerizing show featuring wannabe entrepreneurs with a great product or service who are looking for some assistance both financially and in forming strategic relationships.

The sharks are multimillionaires and billionaires who have persevered and found their way to financial freedom. I am drawn to their insights and their story. At first glance, we see them as greedy and egotistical. But I encourage you to watch it further. Not all are like that. Most seem genuinely interested in hearing the pitch and the idea of each entrepreneur that steps into "The Tank". They are looking to connect, not just to the product or service, but to the person (or team) presenting the idea. They are looking for someone who has persevered and is willing to continue to persevere. That is the *it* factor for them.

If the entrepreneur's idea resonates and if they feel a connection with the person (or team) behind the idea, then invariably one of these sharks is ready to broker a deal.

Sometimes the deal that they offer seems greedy, but more often than not the deal they are willing to offer has some value to the entrepreneur. The deal, to work, must be mutually beneficial.

As my wife and I watch the show, we are intrigued with what the entrepreneur is going to do once an offer is put on the table. Will he or she take up $100K for 33 percent of the company, or will they walk away? My wife and I throw out comments at the entrepreneur as if they are in the room hearing us.

"Take it!" I'll shout.

My wife usually feels the same way, but sometimes her perspective differs, "Are you crazy? She's giving up everything."

But one thing we find compelling is to hear and listen to most of the sharks on the set as they mull things over. They genuinely want to help someone (at least a few of them do). They are looking not just to reinvest and make money, although that's important.

They are looking to infuse and help someone live out a dream. The generosity on that show I find absolutely compelling. In just a half a decade in, there has been over $20 million dollars invested in the entrepreneurs who have been on the show.

A similar show to *Shark Tank* is *The Profit*, which airs on CNBC. *The Profit* features entrepreneur and investor Marcus Lemonis. Marcus's goal is to step into a struggling business and help them back to their feet. He doesn't just write a check; he gives of himself completely to helping initiate a turn around. Investment to him isn't just money—it's his commitment, which starts with a handshake. Behind the scenes, Marcus is also a generous contributor of money and time to a variety of organizations including St. Jude Children's Research Hospital. I believe he's truly a giver!

I am sure there are other shows that are similar to *The Profit* or *Shark Tank*. For me, the takeaway for any of these shows is witnessing the generosity that an influential leader can have for another human being, especially an aspiring entrepreneur or hungry business. Investors, the truly genuine ones, are givers not takers.

Consider that for them to persevere as an entrepreneur, they likely met up with a giver along the way who helped them out. Now that they have found financial freedom, their desire is to play it forward and help others too. Certainly they want to continue to make money, who wouldn't, but the real purpose for gaining wealth is to be able to give it! It is more blessed to give than to receive, that is because, as Francis of Assisi once said, "it is in giving that we receive."

Be Generous with Time and Talent

I was listening to an archived Michael Hyatt podcast one evening on my iPod and something he said caught my attention at the close of the show. He concluded by sharing, "Your life is a gift. Now go make it count."

I sat there for a moment and thought about what he said. My mind then began to reflect on my mother-in-law, Peggie Sue Valentine, who lived this mantra to make life count for others. Peggie was not just my mother-in-law, she was a dear friend and mentor in my life. The love she had for her two daughters and later for her son-in-law's and grandchildren was off the chart. And the love she had for others I don't think could be topped.

In her mid-50s, after working as church secretary for a number of years, she decided she wanted to do more in life. So, she acted on a dream that she quietly held onto for most of her life, a desire to be a nurse.

I will never forget the hard work and determination she put in to become a licensed practical nurse (LPN). I remember Barb and I watching her receive her diploma and celebrating her achievement. It was in amazing accomplishment; we were all very proud.

She was excited too. She couldn't wait to go out and help people—it was her calling in life. After receiving her diploma, she spent the next 12 years of her life dedicated to her profession as a registered nurse. Daily she made an impact with patients and her fellow nurses—touching, sharing, and caring. She would come home always with a smile and often a story. There was no doubt she had found her calling—and she loved it!

In 2008, however, she unfortunately passed away after complications from a stroke. It was devastating. After her passing, we honored her life at the church where she and my father-in-law, Don, attended. While there was mourning, our goal was to celebrate her life and share the great stories. I had a few but mine paled in comparison from the stories her coworkers shared.

Several of them shared how Peggie went above and beyond to help her patients and, even more significantly, help them—a fellow nurse. There were stories about the impact she had not just on the clock, but also off the clock. She would often just talk and engage with someone in need, or sometimes work extra hours uncompensated to cover for someone else who had a family need.

The greatest story, though, came from Sally, a nurse by night but also a mom by day with children to care for on the home front. Sally was about 20 years younger than Peggie, and while she loved her job, she was going through some difficult family struggles. Peggie found out about the challenges and offered to help. But Sally told Peggie that she needed to find a way to work because the money was extremely tight. She went on to share that she would be running out of money before she ran out of month so working the job was critical. Yet, Sally felt the pull to be home and Peggie sensed this. Recognizing the need and the opportunity as most leaders do, Peggie simply smiled and asked, "Why don't you let me take your shift for you?"

Sally at first rejected the idea. Peggie had just worked three nights straight. Peggie needed a break. However, Peggie insisted. She worked that fourth night for Sally without complaint.

In reflecting on the moment, Sally began to get emotional. "It wasn't just that she worked my shift so that I could be at home. She worked that shift for me and gave me her pay for that night so that I could also pay my bills. She never got paid—I did—and she wouldn't have it any other way," said Sally, with tears welling up. I don't think there was a dry eye was in the room.

She then added, "I'll never forget that sacrifice she made for me. That was the most loving thing anybody has have ever done! I'll miss her! We'll all miss her!"

The room was moved. I was moved. Soon a handful of others followed sharing similar stories of her sacrifice and her commitment. Many of them recollected upon the laugh and love that she shared. How she laughed at every joke, but also how she listened to every need and often would give her time and her talents. Simone Well shares that, "Attention is the rarest and purest form of generosity." In that moment, I saw that truth.

I then glanced over Barb, the daughter of this incredible woman whom we were remembering, and saw tears of sadness and joy. In that moment, I realized that while my mother-in-law was gone, her love was not. I realized the blessing of her giving was playing out into eternity. Peggie Valentine was a candle lighter, and even years after her passing, there are still flames lit because of her. And I am one of them!

Author Oswald Sanders once said that, "True greatness, true leadership, is found in giving yourself in service to others." The giving of your time and talent is a powerful means to exhibit generosity. I encourage you to look for those opportunities to share your time and your talents with others to help them persevere too. Let your time and talent be a means to light some candles.

Trait #3 – Be a Team Player

Generosity starts with you—the leader. But to make it last, you want to be part of an organization that is generous too. And that's something you can influence. When you have the right people on the bus—people on your team that share the same values—generosity becomes contagious. To this point, fiction author Jonathan Maberry shares, "Generosity could be as contagious as the zombie plague as long as enough people were willing to be carriers."[72] I laugh at the notion of generosity spreading like a zombie plague, but it's a fun way to think about the potential impact that generosity has on the lives of others. The value that takes place when others exhibit generosity— when they are willing to be carriers— can be contagious. And that's a good thing!

If you have the same desire and like-minded values, you are going to build a team that fits your culture. Here are some questions you might want to consider asking next time you are hiring someone, or looking to partner with someone

- In your last job, what were some ways you were able to meet the needs of your customers? Can you share what were some of those needs, and how you addressed them?

- What are some past experiences and examples that come to mind of how you have helped a colleague or teammate on a project or effort?

- Are there any projects or events that you have particularly enjoyed being a part of outside of the normal job duties that would reveals with us a little more of your passions and interests?

I encourage you to tailor these questions to suit your needs and objectives. Use a tailored version to understand the values of others. Keep in mind that it is hard to be a generous organization if the organization lacks generous people. Since generosity anchors your mission, it should also be part of your team's vision.

Wrap Up

Earlier we talked about the importance of having a desire to make a difference. This is the core foundation to why we should lead. Generosity is at the heart of it. The way that I think about it is that generosity is an external reflection of our internal mission so that we can have an eternal impact. Keep this thought in mind when you pursue your mission.

You'll discover that the fruit of perseverance is in giving. If you see someone who reflects generosity, whether it's through affirmations and encouragement, the sharing of resources, or the offering of time or talent, it may very likely be because they are someone who has learned to persevere themselves.

You are encouraged to adhere to the three traits of a generous leader—

1) Be Humble

2) Be a Role Model

3) Be a Team Player.

Take time also to practice the ART of generosity represented by these three values:

- Affirmations

- Resources

- Time and Talent

Let these values become habits. The benefit to these traits and practices is that when you give you tend to receive. The blessing comes back—it multiplies. I'm not sure exactly how it happens, but it does. That said, I encourage caution as well. Don't just give to receive. That's the wrong motivation. Give to add value to others. Do it because you genuinely care about others. Do it because you can!

I heard it once said that, "If you want to call attention to your good deed then it isn't a good deed, it's a self-serving one."[73] These words, to be honest with you, sting a bit. I've been guilty of giving for the wrong reason. It's a reminder that we shouldn't give because we want to pat ourselves on the back, we should give because we want to help pull someone up. Always remember generosity is the fruit that comes from those who help others press on!

Conclusion -
Finish Strong

In the introduction, I shared the story of Scott Overall, who miraculously won the Peachtree 10K at the last second. The reality is that he would not have reached the finish line if he stopped believing that he could. However, because he believed it was possible, he persevered to the finish. And, because he persevered, he had a chance of winning!

The question to ask ourselves is, *"How will I finish? Will I finish strong – or will I lose hope and not give it my all?"* Asking this question requires you to recognize that you still believe – you still have hope! Recognize that a desire to finish strong coupled with the hope you started with is what should spur you on to persevere.

The Essential Qualities to Lead and Persevere

We have explored four phases to perseverance represented by a simple model: *"Imagine. Create. Explore. Discover."* For each of these phases, we have also examined the various mindset choices that can help leaders and their organizations persevere. These mindset choices represent belief and hope.

If you were to boil down the content of this book into the essential qualities needed to lead and persevere with belief and hope, there are seven.

1) Your Attitude

2) Your Boldness

3) Your Clarity

4) Your Desire

5) Your Engagement

6) Your Faith

7) Your Generosity

Each chapter in this book has tied to at least one of these qualities. As you go back and look at your notes, consider how these qualities can help you persevere.

Recognize that every day we find ourselves staring at a new starting line. It's a new day filled with intrigue and opportunity. How you pursue your day, face your challenges and cross over the starting line is up to you. It's your choice. The challenges that you face, the dreams that you chase, and the struggles you might endure are affected by these seven qualities. Your choices in each of the four phases of the journey are what make a difference.

1) Your position at the start, which is the Imagine Phase. Choose an Attitude of hope. Be Bold. Cast a vision for Clarity. In addition, have Faith in what you believe.

2) Your posture after the gun goes off, which is the Create Phase. Be engaged in growth; let this also reflect your Desire. Use the right systems and tricks to maintain

Clarity. Lead with your Attitude. In addition, stay Bold by calling on courage.

3) Your pace in the middle, which is the Explore Phase. This is when you may encounter "The Dip." When you hit it, just keep going. Your Attitude will help you go beyond yourself. Recognize your Desire is reflected by your passion. Your willingness to improvise, adapt, and overcome both sharpens and exposes your Clarity as well as your Desire. In addition, when you stay inspired it reflects Engagement.

4) Your persistence to the end and beyond, which is the Discover Phase. Your Desire will help you get to the finish, even when the unexpected happens. The experience that you can harvest is a reflection of Engagement with others. It is at this phase that you see your Faith realized. Finally, your Generosity reflects an Attitude of maturity and of a person who perseveres and is willing to help others do so too.

The focus for each of these phases of perseverance boils down to one core question. "How will you finish?" This is important because how you finish tells others how you will lead the next time. Therefore, choose to finish strong!

Despite The Odds, the Impossible Can Happen

I want to close with a personal story that I think reflects one of many scenarios on how the question— "How will you finish?"— can present itself.

Not too long ago, I had a mid-morning flight and I got out of the house a tad on the late side to head to the airport. My wife would tell you that me running late for meeting isn't a surprise, but running late for a flight was a mistake she hoped I'd from learned long ago— but that's another story.

This time around, I was traveling solo. I left the house thinking I was okay on time, but soon after I got the wheels on the pavement, I quickly realized that I might not make my flight. I had about 70 miles of driving ahead of me. The time was 8:30 a.m., and my boarding pass showed a board time of 9:30 a.m. not 10:00 a.m. like I had thought earlier. I was off by a half hour, just in planning.

I quickly calculated that the chance of making my flight was about as likely as me walking on water. It was next to impossible. I fumbled for my phone, and asked Siri to search for the phone number for JetBlue. After a few failed attempts, I got the number and reached reservations.

"Hi, my name is Sally, welcome to JetBlue reservation center."

I was relieved to get a live voice instead of a robot. She continued, "How can I help you?"

Surprisingly, in a calm, non-frantic voice I introduce myself and shared my plight. "Hi, my name is Paul, and I have a flight this morning out of Richmond. But, to be honest, I am not sure I'm going to make it on time."

Now, my phone was Bluetooth connected to my dashboard, so she was likely hearing road noise, and passing trucks as I entered on the highway.

"Okay," she replied, "Just for clarity, did you say you have a flight this morning that you don't think you will make?" She paused briefly. "Do you need me to cancel your flight?"

I quickly responded. "Well, I want to see if there is a later flight that I can catch?"

I could hear Sally draw in a deep breath as she clicked on her mouse. "Let me see what we can do for you." After some tapping on her keyboard, she added, "Can you provide me your reservation code or e-ticket number?"

I quickly gave her my reservation number.

After a few more seconds of typing she came back. "Okay—I see you have a flight out of Richmond at 10 a.m. The next flight I can put you on is a 1:30 p.m. flight to Boston, and then a flight from Boston that will get you into Orlando at 9:47 tonight."

She paused long enough for me to take it in, and then came back with the question I expected. "Do you want me to change your flight to this later flight? Or..." She paused, "Do you want to see if you can make it to the flight you currently have a reservation for?"

I looked at the clock. It was 8:44 a.m. I tried to imagine myself boarding the plane in just over forty-five minutes, even though I still had about sixty miles in front of me.

"Well, I suppose I can try to catch my current flight." I responded. Then I asked, "If I don't make it, will this other flight be an option? I can decide then, right?"

After a moment, she responded. "Yes. I suggest though you try to catch the flight you're booked on now. But if you don't make it—then, yes—we will put you on the other flight."

Then, to emphasize the urgency of my situation, she added, "But keep in mind there's a fifty-dollar change fee. And you won't have the direct flight you are booked on now."

"Okay, thanks. I guess I am going to see if I can make my current flight."

"Okay, very good. Hope you make it." She then ended with, "Thank you for calling JetBlue."

"Thanks for your help," I said, as I felt the pressure rising.

After I hung up the phone, I looked up through my sunroof and muttered six words to the heavens. "I am looking for a miracle."

I then pondered my arrow prayer. "Do I think it's possible? Can a miracle really happen? Do miracles still happen?" I looked at my speed, my clock, and the distance I had to go.

Then a thought hit me. "Why couldn't miracles still happen?"

However, my analytical mind said, "There was just no way. It's impossible."

But my heart countered just a little louder, "You've got to try. You won't know until you do."

My mind went into Spock mode as I tried to guesstimate times I needed to hit certain mile markers and land marks. I first calculated that I needed to have King's Dominion, an amusement park along the way, in my sights by 9:00 a.m.

As the clock got closer to nine, I held out hope. "Would I see it?" I wondered aloud. When nine o'clock came, I was still one exit away. King's Dominion was still a few miles down range, so I missed that initial target time.

Finally, at 9:05 a.m., I saw the park's replica of the Eiffel Tower. I realized, "Okay—I am off by five minutes."

I then transitioned that thought to a statement of frustration. "Man, if only I left five minutes earlier."

The conversation I continued with myself was less than pleasant. I began verbally beating myself up. Fortunately, I quickly pushed those thoughts away otherwise I could have quickly spiraled down to helplessness. I had to shake off the doubt, "No. You cannot change the past, but you can change the future. Keep going! You've got to press on!"

I then speculated that I needed to hit the I-295 interchange no later than 9:12 a.m. That was in just seven minutes. Traffic started getting a little thicker. My speed dropped. I watched 9:12 a.m. quickly slip by. It wasn't until 9:18 a.m. that I hit the I-295 interchange around Richmond. I was now six minutes off my self-imposed drop-dead time to make my flight.

I started thinking about the elements of pressing on, the patterns of perseverance. I realized that this was a test. I looked back up through the sunroof to fire off one more arrow prayer.

"God, I am still looking for a miracle. I'm asking you to take my mistake and do your thing because I'm just going to believe nothing is impossible." Then aloud I added, "Let's do this!" I was counting on faith at this point.

At 9:28 a.m., I reached the turn off to head to the airport. In front of me was a three-mile drive. During that time, I created an internal checklist that I needed to execute once I arrived to the airport.

- ☐ Park
- ☐ Remember my parking spot
- ☐ Grab my stuff
- ☐ Lock the Car
- ☐ Head to the terminal
- ☐ Have my boarding pass ready
- ☐ Show my ID
- ☐ Get through security
- ☐ Run to the gate

Then I added a thought to my checklist that almost killed my momentum and my spirit.

- ☐ Watch the door to the gate close just as I get there
- ☐ Watch the plane pulling away from the jet bridge

I started thinking, "There's no way."

Deep within me, the voice came back. "Don't you think you've got to try? Don't give up. Remember, leaders press on."

Finally, I pulled into the parking garage at 9:35 a.m. and drove up to the second deck. As I turned and headed toward the terminal, a convenient, perfect spot appeared. It was a sign of hope, which I needed.

I quickly jumped out and grabbed my gear. After taking a quick picture of the parking spot, I ran toward the terminal. Then, I discovered I was parked on the level that I could just walk across a bridge (run, really) into to the airport and the terminal. No elevators.

No stairs. I ran toward the gate only to find a long security line. My heart sank.

I looked at my watch. It was 9:40 a.m. "Wow," I thought. "So close. Amazing that I'm here, but this line is so long." I pondered, "How can I make it?"

Only one TSA person was checking boarding passes and identifications. Just as I started thinking I might have to switch to that later flight through Boston, another miracle happened. A new TSA agent came from nowhere, and opened a new line. In less than sixty seconds, he was scanning my boarding pass and ID. I was through security ninety seconds later!

I quickly grabbed my shoes and jumped back into them. Running with my jacket half on, I sprinted what seemed like a mile to Gate 10. As I got closer, I saw a woman ahead of me scrambling to the door as well. They let her through, which was another sign of hope.

When I got to the gate, the agent at the desk looked up at me and simply said my name.

"Paul?" No last name. Just my first name.

I quickly responded, "Yes."

He said, "I don't need your boarding pass—I got you. Go on," he said with a smile.

Before I knew it, I found myself on the jet bridge with my suitcase and laptop bag. I got to the entry of the plane and met the pilot and flight attendant who were standing there. With a warm smile, they welcomed me. Then they looked at my bag and said,

"I'm afraid that's not going to fit. We are going to need to check it. Is that okay?"

I responded, "Do you still have time?"

The pilot laughed. "Yes—just barely. You can pick it up at baggage claim once you arrive in Orlando."

I thanked him and quickly went to my seat. I plopped down and took a huge deep breath. I could not believe it. I had actually made it. Then I looked at my watch. It was 9:51 a.m.

I shook my head. Logically I shouldn't have been there. But I was. I was on the plane. I had made it!

Then I wondered what my day would have been like if I hadn't persevered? What if I hadn't pressed on?

Then it came to me—I wouldn't have experienced a miracle.

In that moment of relief and reflection, I grabbed a pen from my bag and wrote a thought down on the back of a business card; a thought that I hope I will always remember, "When leaders press on, despite the odds, the impossible can happen!"

Afterword

Since I began writing this book, I have experienced some interesting opportunities and challenges that have allowed me to put these principles to practice once again. Life provides its share of tests, and through them I am continuing to learn the beauty in persevering.

Shortly after I begin writing this book, I experienced partial vision loss in my left eye—a condition called optic neuritis. In an effort to further determine the extent of my problem, I was diagnosed with something I never saw coming—multiple sclerosis; better known as MS. Needless to say that diagnosis gave me quite a shock, but it has only heightened my awareness of all that life has to offer. I have come to realize that, to make the most of life, I need to persevere. After all, what do I have to lose? Our quality of life is not just in what is given to us, it's in what we give back to it. Challenges are best experienced by those who are willing to press on.

Recently, I was reminded of another intimidating time when my business partners, Larry and Steve, and I thought we were going to be fired from our day job. We were just six months in from starting the new business of SimVentions. We were working nights and weekends on our startup, and by day we were maintaining employment with the company that held our day job. We worked diligently to maintain the separation. In addition, to maintain integrity, we shared with the leadership at our day job of our entrepreneur start up that we were working in the off hours. A few weeks later, the owner of the company flew down and specifically asked to meet with the three of us. When we were summoned for the meeting, we thought it might be the end.

Part of me was nervous and concerned. I didn't like the idea of losing my day job, which was providing a steady income for me and my family. I didn't want to leave my family high and dry. The thought crossed each of our minds to perhaps walk into the meeting prepared to announce that we were putting our business pursuit on hold, and to simply ask for grace so that we could stay gainfully employed.

However, we decided just before the meeting we would not yet give up, and we prepared ourselves mentally and prayerfully for the consequence of our decision no matter what that might be. The moments you don't know what to expect next are the ones you often remember—they result in opportunities to persevere.

As we settled into our seats and exchanged our pleasantries, the owner of the company, a leader we all admired, shared that his purpose for the meeting was to better understand our mission, and get clarity of our vision for our startup. After we shared with him our intent and desire, he responded not by firing us, but instead offering his support.

His remarks to us where unforgettable: "Now that I understand your intent, I want to extend my support—my blessing." He continued, with a level of enthusiasm that we hadn't anticipated, "I am truly excited for you! I remember being right where you were at less than twenty years earlier. You have a vision just as I had one. You should pursue it just as I did. Far be it from me to stop you. Instead, I want to encourage you. Continue here as long as you need to, you have my support so long as you keep me in the loop."

Talk about being blown away. That meeting turned from dread to exhilaration in less than an hour; it was a tremendous encouragement to us. Big dreams may cause big concerns, but they also create great opportunities.

Shortly after that conversation, I remember driving by a beautiful office building that had just been vacated right off of Interstate 95. It was a spectacular place, and I allowed myself to imagine for a moment our company one day occupying space in that building. I also imagined our name on the side of the building for all to see. Later, I shared my dream with Steve and Larry. We agreed how incredible it would be and ended the conversation with "maybe one day." It was a discussion that almost was forgotten, until recently.

Due to our limited budget in those early days, our first bold move was into a low priced office space just south of town in the offices of an old manufacturing plant. It was small. It was cramped. The location wasn't ideal, but it was ours. The only problem was that we didn't have steady revenue yet and, in those early days, we wondered how in the world we were going to pay for the $650 a month rent. While we had the promise of new work, which was the basis for signing the lease, it had not come in yet. The moment was scary. Fortunately, within just a few months, we got through it and grew from three to four. We persevered, and God provided.

A year later, we found ourselves with eight employees and ready for a bigger place. So, we leased a new space seven times larger than we were presently located. Then, in just two years' time, we outgrew that place too—now with twenty-one employees. We needed to move again.

Now, as I write this afterword, we have just completed our fourth move into a bigger space to accommodate our over 200 employees. And this time you won't believe where are now located! It's in the building that we imagined fifteen years earlier right off Interstate 95. Today, our main offices sit in that location with our name on the side easily seen day and night by motorists that pass by.

The fact that we are in this building is a testament of both perseverance and God's provision. Each time we have moved into a new space it has been a step of faith and it can be a challenge, each time God has responded in a significant way, whether it's the addition of great work or great people. I believe that when you strive to honor God a blessing is returned.

I heard it once said that dreams come a size too big so that we can grow into them. For me, for my business, for the church I attend, for the organization I support, and for my friends and family, I have found this to be true. The only way to know how big the dream really is to persevere and find out!

Start with the model *"Imagine. Create. Explore. Discover."* Then leverage the mindset choices described in this book. If you do, I believe you will find that the power of perseverance will make a difference in your life and in others.

Acknowledgements

While this book may have my name as the author, it has not been a solo effort. Any act of perseverance usually requires a team. And this book is no exception.

There are a number of individuals I want to thank; individuals who have been leaders in my life that have inspired me to dream more, learn more, do more, and become more!

First, the inspiration that I found where I discovered and observed many of the patterns of perseverance came primarily from my family—especially my dad and my two boys, Michael and Ryan. By now, you have read about Michael. Ryan, my youngest son, inspires me with his creativity and intuition of how things work and then being able to explain it. It's a real gift. He has the insight of my uncle, Jay Kershaw, and, like his brother, someone I can see doing amazing things. Michael and Ryan, I can't wait to see the impact you both can make to the world.

My wife, Barbara, is truly an inspiration to me too. Thank you for persevering with me and believing in me. Thanks for speaking life into me all those years ago. I'll always remember, "You still have hope, don't you?" Those are still words of life to me!

There is also my mom, sister, and brother. Mom, Kathy, and Kurt, thank you for inspiring me. Dad was an inspiration for all of us, and this book is in honor of him. I hope I was able to bring a portion of his wisdom to life.

I am thankful for the amazing help of my writing advisor, Stephanie Wetzel; my editor, Michelle Labor; and my proofreaders, Tom Howard and Chris Jones. Thank you for the time and effort you put in reviewing, suggesting, editing and reviewing again the content for this book. Other reviewers of earlier excerpts and supporters of this book include Annie Brock, James Bauslaugh, Joseph Dutkiewicz, Nathan Eckel, Bob and Nancy Kittridge, Mike Lightner, Tony Lynch, Mark McAuliffe, Rick Miller, and Tom Telesco. You all have helped make these pages clearer, more poignant, and more impactful.

There are many other people who encourage and inspire me as well, whom I want to thank: my SimVentions leadership partners Larry Root, Steve Goss, George Hughes, Bob Duffy, Joe Caliri, Herb Kaler, and Matt Wilson. It's an honor to lead with you guys! And to all the gang at SimVentions, thank you! You guys are amazing! Every day I come to work and I am inspired because of the perseverance and passion you give for our customers, our community, and each other!

One person that has modeled perseverance for me over the past two years at work is Roger Booker. Roger you have been through a lot, but you keep on fighting. You keep getting back up no matter what. Thanks for showing all of us how these qualities of perseverance—attitude, boldness, clarity, desire, engagement, faith, and generosity—truly make a difference; especially faith.

Special thanks to Mike Harbour, Barry Smith, Dave Gambrill, and Bill Buckingham for your support from the start. Thanks to Steven Apicella who has always been a supporter for the past two decades. Thanks also to my long distance friend, Doug Taylor, who has been a huge support for me over the past ten years. Doug, I appreciate those "I'm praying for you!" messages that God prompts you to send!

I want to thank some other great mentors, leaders, and coaches in my life too: John Maxwell, Paul Martinelli, Scott Fay, Mark Cole, Ed DeCosta, Melissa West, Roddy Galbraith, and Christian Simpson. I am truly humbled and honored to know and learn from each of you.

There are many—many—with the John Maxwell Team who have been part of my support group. I want to name each of you, but I'm afraid I'll miss someone (or run out of ink). Please know how much you have meant to me during this time. Thank you for your support.

I also want to thank my pastor, Daniel Floyd, not just for the foreword you wrote, but for the weekly inspiration on Sundays and the times we've connected over a cup of coffee along the way. Lifepoint Church is no doubt a place where people like me can get our candle lit each and every week. Pastor Daniel, thank you for your encouragement.

Also a shout out to the great authors and leaders who took time to chat with me and inspired me over the last few years as part of The Platform Builders. Thank you for your time and influence. In particular, I want to mention Michael Hyatt, Dr. Henry Cloud, Simon Sinek, Dr. Kathy Cramer, Adam Grant and Mark Miller. It was more than just your conversation that I had with you; it was the impact you made well long after.

I'd like to thank Captain Eugene "Red" McDaniel, US Navy (Retired), and his family for allowing me to retell a brief part of his story. Red, your courage and faith was an inspiration to my dad and is still an inspiration to us all.

I want to give a shout out to the Fort Hunt High School class of 1984, and special thanks to Coach Windsor, Marc Lerro, and all of my other track teammates. You guys changed my world.

Thanks also to Jack Bergen and Bill Kompare. Thanks for believing in those you lead.

There are many others that I'd also like to mention, but the hour is late and I'm ready to push save—spare two more acknowledgements that I have to make!

I want to acknowledge and thank my Lord and Savior, Jesus Christ. Thank you for Your patience with me, and for Your grace and mercy. Thank you for allowing me to be an instrument to capture and share with others how perseverance can tell our story. You have revealed to me that our story is really Your story of love, endurance, and triumph.

Finally, to you the readers—thank you for picking up this book and giving it a read. That means the world to me. I hope it adds value. I would love to hear from you. Find me on Twitter, or the web link below. Let me know how this book has encouraged you to press on!

Paul Gustavson
@PaulGustavson
www.leaderspresson.com

Notes

[1] Scott Overall, @scottoverall, Twitter, https://twitter.com/scottoverall/status/617334933388980224, July 4, 2015.

[2] *"Imagine. Create. Explore. Discover. ™"* is a trademark of SimVentions, Inc., first used January 2000.

[3] James 1:2-4, New International Version.

[4] Kary Oberbrunner, *Deeper Path, The: Five Steps That Let Your Hurts Lead to Your Healing*, p. 29, Baker Publishing Group, 2013.

[5] John Maxwell, *Developing the Leader Within You*, Thomas Nelson, 2012.

[6] Eugene Red McDaniel, *Scars and Stripes: The True Story of One Man's Courage Facing Death as a POW in Vietnam*, p. 26, Midpoint Trade Books, 2012.

[7] *Ibid*, p. 40.

[8] *Ibid*, pp. 40-41.

[9] Quote is commonly attributed to Benjamin Mays who was an American Baptist minister, activist in the African-American Civil Rights Movement.

[10] Michael Nelson, *The Evolving Presidency: Landmark Documents*, 1787-2015, SAGE Publication, 2015.

[11] Martin Luther King, Jr., *I Have a Dream*, delivered at the Lincoln Memorial, Washington D.C., 28 August 1963.

[12] Scott M. Fay, *Discover Your Sweet Spot: The 7 Steps to Create a Life of Success and Significance*, p. 14, Morgan James Publishing. Kindle Edition, 2013.

[13] SimVentions, Purpose, Vision and Mission, visible online at www.simventions.com.

[14] Winston Churchill, Speech at Kinnaird Hall, Dundee, Scotland ("Unemployment"), 10 October 1908.

[15] Mother Teresa of Calcutta, An address at the National Prayer Breakfast (Sponsored by the U.S. Senate and House of Representatives), February 3, 1994. – also watch (start at 8:45): https://www.youtube.com/watch?v=OXn-wf5ylgo.

[16] Paul Williams, *Mother Teresa*. Indianapolis. Alpha Books, pp. 199–204. ISBN 0-02-864278-3, 2002.

[17] Martin Luther King, Jr., His Last Speech, April 3, 1968, at the Mason Temple (Church of God in Christ Headquarters) in Memphis, Tennessee. The next day, King was assassinated. Start at 1:51 https://www.youtube.com/watch?v=4WZbxYGy3As.

₁₈ Jeremiah 29:11, New International Version.

[19] Robert Burns, *To a Mouse*, Poem, November 1785.

[20] Thought based on a quote attributed to Marvin Phillips. He said, "The difference between try and triumph is a little umph."

[21] Quote is commonly attributed to Rikki Rogers. Rikki is a graphic artist. You can find her on Twitter @rikkirogers.

[22] George Washington, *The Rules of Civility*, http://www.mountvernon.org.

[23] Thomas Jefferson, http://tjrs.monticello.org/letter/1424.

[24] Steve Jobs, Stanford Commencement Address, June 12, 2005.

[25] John Wayne, http://johnwayne.com/legacy/quotes/.

[26] *Deja Vu*, Touchstone Pictures, 2006.

[27] "8 Jules Verne Inventions That Came True (Pictures)", National Geographic Online, photo gallery, http://bit.ly/JulesVerneInventions, last accessed Dec 29, 2015.

[28] "Leonardo da Vinci Inventions," http://bit.ly/DaVinciInventions, last accessed December 29, 2015.

[29] James 1:6, New International Version.

[30] Proverbs 29:18, New International Version.

[31] Bill Bryson, *Neither Here nor There*, Doubleday, September 2012.

[32] Seth Godin, *Poke the Box*. Amazon Encore. Kindle Edition, 2011.

[33] John C. Maxwell, as shared at the International Maxwell Training, West Palm Beach, Florida, February 2002.

[34] John C. Maxwell, *Good Leaders Ask Great Questions: Your Foundation for Successful Leadership,* Kindle Locations 1404-1405, Center Street. Kindle Edition, 2014.

[35] Ed Catmull and Amy Wallace, *Creativity, Inc.: Overcoming the Unseen Forces That Stand in the Way of True Inspiration*, Kindle Location 144, Random House, 2014.

[36] David Allen, *Getting Things Done Productivity Cards*, 2013.

[37] Douglas Graham and Thomas T. Bachmann, *Ideation: The Birth and Death of Ideas*, p. 54, John Wiley and Sons Inc., 2004.

[38] Roger Brown, *Multitasking Gets You There Later*, https://www.infoq.com/articles/multitasking-problems, June 20, 2010, last accessed June 4, 2016.

[39] Dr. Henry Cloud, Henry, *Boundaries for Leaders (Enhanced Edition): Results, Relationships, and Being Ridiculously In Charge*, p. 135, HarperCollins. Kindle Edition, 2013.

[40] Scott Fay, *Discover Your Sweet Spot: The 7 Steps to Create a Life of Success and Significance*, p. 18, Morgan James Publishing. Kindle Edition, 2013.

[41] https://en.wiktionary.org/wiki/actor#Etymology_5 and also https://en.wiktionary.org/wiki/Ἄκτωρ, last accessed May 28, 2016.

[42] Felix Baumgartner Web Site, http://www.redbullstratos.com/the-team/felix-baumgartner/, last accessed June 4, 2016.

[43] Dina Spector, "Felix Baumgartner's Biggest Fear: His Own Space Suit", *Business Insider*, October 9, 2012, http://bit.ly/Baumgartner-Biggest-Fear.

[44] Andrew S. Grove, *Only the Paranoid Survive: How to Exploit the Crisis Points That Challenge Every Company*, Kindle Location 974, The Crown Publishing Group, Kindle Edition, 2010.

[45] *ibid*, Kindle Location 1139.

[46] Matt Damon as "Mark Watney", *The Martian*, Twentieth Century Fox, 2015.

[47] Seth Godin, *"The Dip: A Little Book That Teaches You When to Quit (and When to Stick)"*, p. 17, Penguin Publishing Group. Kindle Edition, 2007.

[48] Jim Collins, *"Good to Great: Why Some Companies Make the Leap...And Others Don't"*, Kindle Locations 203-204. HarperCollins. Kindle Edition, 2011.

[49] Louis Zamperini and David Rensin, *Don't Give Up, Don't Give In: Lessons from an Extraordinary Life*, p. 71. HarperCollins. Kindle Edition, 2014.

[50] *ibid*, p. 34.

[51] Nick Vujicic, *Your Life Without Limits: Living Above Your Circumstances*, Kindle Locations 29-31, The Doubleday Religious Publishing Group, Kindle Edition, 2012.

[52] *Ibid*, Kindle Location 154.

[53] Quote commonly attributed to Robert Collier who wrote "Success is the sum of small efforts repeated day in and day out."

[54] "Improvise, Adapt and Overcome" – A mantra that symbolizes the flexibility, resourcefulness and quick decision-making ability found throughout the Marine ranks, http://www.marines.com/history-heritage/traditions.

[55] Charles Duhigg, *The Power of Habit: Why We Do What We Do in Life and Business*, Kindle Locations 434-435, Random House Publishing Group. Kindle Edition, 2012.

[56] Kathryn Cramer, *Lead Positive: What Highly Effective Leaders See, Say, and Do*, Kindle Locations 302-303, Wiley, Kindle Edition, 2014.

[57] Alice Lipscombe-Southwell. "30 Most Innovative Business Leaders of 2013," http://www.business-management-degree.net/30-innovative-business-leaders-2013/, last accessed January 13, 2016.

[58] Conversations with Dr. Kathy Cramer, The Platform Builders, July 2014.

[59] Tad Friend, *Plugged In*, "Can Elon Musk lead the way to an electric-car future?", http://bit.ly/ElonMusk2009, posted 2009, last accessed May 29, 2016.

[60] Quote is often attributed to Samuel Johnson.

[61] Ephesians 4:12, New International Version.

[62] The idea of turning inspiration into perspiration was seeded by a comment by Darren Hardy in his sharing of his book *The Entrepreneur Roller Coaster*, 2015.

[63] Charlie Peacock, "Experience, *"The Secret of Time,* 1990.

[64] Russell Crow as "Maximus", *Gladiator*, Universal Pictures, 2000.

[65] Joyce Meyer, *Closer to God Each Day: 365 Devotions for Everyday Living*, p. 358, FaithWords. Kindle Edition, 2015.

[66] Brad Lomenick, *H3 Leadership: Be Humble. Stay Hungry. Always Hustle*, p. 45, Thomas Nelson. Kindle Edition, 2015.

[67] Charles Duhigg, *The Power of Habit: Why We Do What We Do in Life and Business*, Kindle Location 1384, Random House Publishing Group, Kindle Edition, 2012.

[68] A variant of this quote is commonly attributed to Will Rogers.

[69] Sharon Salzberg, *The Real Power of Generosity*, http://www.onbeing.org/blog/the-real-power-of-generosity/7489

[70] Maia Szalavitz, *Humility: A Quiet, Underappreciated Strength*, Time, http://bit.ly/HumblePeople, posted April 13, 2012, last accessed May 29, 2016.

[71] Russell Razzaque M.D., *Learning Humility From Lincoln*, Psychology Today, http://bit.ly/LincolnHumility, Posted April 10, 2012, last accessed May 29, 2016.

[72] Jonathan Maberry, *Dust & Decay*, Simon & Schuster Books, Sept 2012.

[73] Quote is commonly attributed to author Donna Lynn Hope.

About the Author

Paul Gustavson is a cofounder of SimVentions, and a founding partner of the John Maxwell Team. SimVentions, is located in Fredericksburg, Virginia, and has been recognized as one of Virginia's Best Places to Work, and recently named by Inc. Magazine as one of "The 50 Best Places to Work in 2016". As the Chief Technology Officer (CTO), Paul leads in identifying and contributing to the company's capability and influencing the strategic vision.

He is a connector and pioneer focused on innovative and relevant ideas that can make an impact. He has also written for numerous journals and several technical books, presents and speaks at conferences domestically and internationally. Paul and his wife live in Virginia.

Additional Resources and Information

- Additional resources for *Leaders Press On* are available at www.leaderspresson.com.

- To learn more about SimVentions, visit www.simventions.com.